The ABAP® Quick Reference

SAP PRESS and the SAP PRESS Essentials are issued
by Bernhard Hochlehnert, SAP AG

SAP PRESS is a joint initiative of SAP and Galileo Press. The know-how offered by SAP specialists combined with the expertise of the publishing house Galileo Press offers the reader expert books in the field. SAP PRESS features first-hand information and expert advice, and provides useful skills for professional decision-making.

SAP PRESS offers a variety of books on technical and business related topics for the SAP user. For further information, please visit our website: www.sap-press.com.

Horst Keller
The Official ABAP Reference
2-Volume Set with 3 CDs
2nd Ed. 2005, 1216 pp., ISBN 1-59229-039-6

Heuvelmans, Krouwels, Meijs, Sommen
Enhancing the Quality
of ABAP Development
2004, 504 pp., ISBN 1-59229-030-2

Frédéric Heinemann, Christian Rau
Web Programming in ABAP
with the SAP Web Application Server
2nd Ed. 2005, 596 pp., ISBN 1-59229-060-4

Brochhausen, Kielisch, Schnerring, Staeck
mySAP HR—Technical Principles and Programming
2nd Ed. 2005, approx. 450 pp., ISBN 1-59229-055-8

Horst Keller

The ABAP® Quick Reference

SAP PRESS is an imprint of Galileo Press,
Fort Lee (NJ), USA
Bonn, Germany

German Edition first published 2005 by Galileo Press.

Translation Lemoine International, Inc., Salt Lake City, UT
Copy Editor John Parker, UCG, Inc., Boston, MA
Cover Design Silke Braun
Printed in Germany

ISBN 1-59229-057-4

Contents

Preface

In the context of my work on ABAP documentations and publications during the past 10 years I often have been asked what had happened to the good old ABAP reference card and if there were plans to publish anything similar in the future. The old hands among you might remember that in the R/2 days there used to be a folding card that contained the ABAP commands available at that time, important transaction codes, and some additional information. And even though it was no longer up-to-date, this folding card was reprinted from time to time for use with the R/3 system.

It has since become impossible to fit all the ABAP and ABAP Objects statements onto a folding card, which is why I want to provide all those who have asked me about it—and, of course, all other ABAP developers too—with this ABAP Quick Reference. I hope it is a worthy successor to the card. Although you won't find any list of transaction codes in it, the book contains other tables with ABAP-related information as well as the complete short description of the transformation language ST.

As always, I would like to say thank you to all my colleagues in the *SAP NetWeaver Developer Tools ABAP* team and their manager, Andreas Blumenthal, at SAP AG. Without this team and their support, a lot of what I do—if not all of it—would be impossible. And again, I'd like to express my gratitude to my student assistant Agnieszka Chelminska who spotted a multitude of mistakes in the final page proof right at the very last minute. At Galileo Press I'd like to thank my editors Florian Zimniak and Stefan Proksch, who once again have helped me turn an idea into a project; thanks also to Vera Brauner and Steffi Ehrentraut for turning the manuscript into this attractive book format. Last, but not least, I'd like to express my deepest gratitude to my wife Ute for once again having sacrificed many hours of our free time for the sake of this book project.

Walldorf, Germany, July 2005
Horst Keller

Introduction

The ABAP Quick Reference is intended for all ABAP programmers who have a sound knowledge of ABAP and need to quickly look up the syntax of an ABAP statement or the meaning of an addition during their daily work. The book also addresses all those who want to get a quick overview of ABAP.

Furthermore, this Quick Reference is the ideal companion to The Official ABAP Reference Book, also published by SAP PRESS. In contrast to the ABAP Reference Book, this Quick Reference does not—with a few exceptions—contain any pseudo syntax. The Quick Reference shows almost all the syntax diagrams in their full extent so that the additions to a statement and their basic meaning become clear at a glance. Pseudo syntax is only used in a few cases where multiple statements use the same extensive syntax and a full display of it would lead to a loss of clarity, for instance with logical expressions or SQL conditions. In the syntax diagrams, pseudo syntax is italicized.

In addition to the statements of the ABAP programming language, this Quick Reference contains statements of the dynpro flow logic and, as a bonus, the statements for Simple Transformations.

For all information that goes beyond the short descriptions given in this Quick Reference—such as the exact semantics of a language element, the types of operands, potential exceptions, and the embedding into the environment—please refer to the The Official ABAP Reference Book. This holds true particularly for the terminology used in the Quick Reference, as you can generally find all terms in the glossary of the ABAP Reference Book.

Overview

The ABAP Quick Reference is made up of three parts. Each of these three parts contains the syntax descriptions of one of the three SAP-specific programming languages that play an essential role on the SAP NetWeaver Application Server ABAP (SAP NW AS ABAP).

- **ABAP**

  ABAP (*Advanced Business Application Programming*) and its integrated enhancement ABAP Objects together represent the programming interface of SAP NW AS ABAP in SAP NetWeaver. The application logic and almost all the services of an ABAP-based SAP system are programmed in ABAP. ABAP programs are created with the ABAP Editor, which can be used either as an independent application or as an add-on to other tools such as Object Navigator or Class Builder. The syntax diagrams of the ABAP statements and the corresponding short descriptions make up the first and biggest part of this Quick Reference.

- **Dynpro**

  Dynpros (*Dynamic Programs*) are the basis for programming classical user interfaces for ABAP programs in SAP GUI. A dynpro is always a component of an ABAP program. It consists of a *screen layout* and a *dynpro flow logic*. You can create general dynpros using the Screen Painter tool. Specific dynpros such as selection screens and list dynpros are created implicitly. Even today, classical dynpros are still widely used, although their importance will rapidly decrease in the future due to the introduction of Web Dynpro for ABAP. Programming Web Dynpro for ABAP doesn't require any specific language and can be done using ABAP Objects. The small set of statements of the classical dynpro flow logic forms the second part of the Quick Reference.

- **ST**

  ST (*Simple Transformation*) is a language used to transform ABAP data to XML and vice versa. Since Release 6.40, SAP's proprietary ST can be used as an alternative to standardized XSLT, for which a processor has been an integral part of the ABAP runtime environment since Release 6.10. In contrast to XSLT, the ST language doesn't require the specific asXML format (*ABAP Serialization XML*). You can create simple transformations using the Transformation

Builder tool. The third part of this Quick Reference contains the syntax diagrams of all the currently available ST statements.

In addition to the description of statements, the Quick Reference also contains tables at the ends of the ABAP and ST sections with lists of important designators and special characters.

Releases Used

The Quick Reference deals with all ABAP, dynpro, and ST language elements up to and including the Release 7.0, the latest release. Release-specific changes as of Release 4.6 have been marked accordingly. The following table lists the assignments of the release names used in this book to the names used by SAP for their technology components; it also names some SAP applications that are based on these releases.

Release name	Technology component	SAP applications
None*	SAP Basis 4.6	SAP R/3 4.6C, SAP APO 3.1, ...
6.10	SAP Web Application Server 6.10	CRM 3.0, ...
6.20	SAP Web Application Server 6.20/6.30	SAP R/3 Enterprise 4.70, CRM 3.1, SCM 4.0, SAP KW 6.0, ...
6.40	SAP Web Application Server 6.40 in SAP NetWeaver 04	mySAP ERP 2004, CRM 4.0, SCM 4.1, ...
7.0	SAP NetWeaver Application Server ABAP 7.0 in SAP NetWeaver 2004s	mySAP Business Suite and xApps 2005

* If no name is specified in ST statements, then this corresponds to Release 6.40 as ST wasn't introduced until this release.

ABAP Statements

This part lists all ABAP statements in alphabetical order except for statements and additions for internal use. Obsolete statements and additions are marked accordingly.

ADD

Syntax

```
ADD dobj1 TO dobj2.
```

Effect

Adds the content of a numerical data object `dobj1` to the content of a numerical data object `dobj2` and assigns the result to `dobj2`.

ADD-CORRESPONDING

Syntax

```
ADD-CORRESPONDING struc1 TO struc2.
```

Release

Obsolete

Effect

Adds the components of a structure `struc1` to components having the same name of a structure `struc2`.

ADD—THEN, UNTIL

Syntax

```
ADD { { dobj1 THEN dobj2 UNTIL dobj
      { {TO result} | {GIVING result [ACCORDING TO sel]} } }
    | { dobj FROM pos1 TO pos GIVING result } }
    [RANGE range].
```

Release

Obsolete

Effect
Adds up sequences of data objects that are stored in the memory in equal intervals.

Additions
- `THEN ... UNTIL`
  Defines the sequence by means of the interval between the data objects `dobj1` and `dobj2`.
- `TO result`
  Adds the result to the content of `result`.
- `GIVING result`
  Assigns the result to `result`.
- `FROM ... TO`
  Defines the sequence by means of data objects that directly follow each other in the memory, the first one being `dobj`, and the elements of which are determined by `pos1` and `pos`.
- `ACCORDING TO sel`
  Restricts the elements of a sequence with the conditions of a selection table.

Addition since Release 6.10
- `RANGE range`
  Limits the addressable memory area to the `range` structure.

aggregate

Syntax

```
{ MAX( [DISTINCT] col )
| MIN( [DISTINCT] col )
| AVG( [DISTINCT] col )
| SUM( [DISTINCT] col )
| COUNT( DISTINCT col )
| COUNT( * )
| count(*) }
```

Effect
Aggregate expressions in the `SELECT` statement.

Additions
- `MAX( [DISTINCT] col )`
  Maximum value of the values in the `col` column.

- `MIN( [DISTINCT] col )`
  Minimum value of the values in the `col` column.
- `AVG( [DISTINCT] col )`
  Average value of the values in the `col` column.
- `SUM( [DISTINCT] col )`
  Sum of the values in the `col` column.
- `COUNT( DISTINCT col )`
  Number of different values in the `col` column.
- `COUNT( * ), count(*)`
  Number of rows in the resulting set.

ALIASES

Syntax

```
ALIASES alias FOR intf~comp.
```

Effect

Declares an alias name `alias` for a component `comp` of the interface `intf` in a class or an interface.

APPEND

Syntax

```
APPEND { wa
       | {INITIAL LINE}
       | {LINES OF jtab [FROM idx1] [TO idx2]} }
   TO itab [SORTED BY comp]
   [ {ASSIGNING <fs> [CASTING]} | {REFERENCE INTO dref} ].
```

Effect

Appends lines to an internal table `itab`.

Additions

- `wa`
  Appends a work area `wa`.
- `INITIAL LINE`
  Appends an initial line.
- `LINES OF jtab [FROM idx1] [TO idx2]`
  Appends lines from `idx1` through `idx2` from the internal table `jtab`.

- SORTED BY comp
  Creates a ranking list in descending order sorted by the line component comp.

Additions since Release 6.10

- ASSIGNING <fs>
  Assigns an appended single line to a field symbol <fs>.
- REFERENCE INTO dref
  Sets a data reference dref to an appended single line.

Addition since Release 7.0

- CASTING
  Casts the line to the typing of the field symbol.

ASSERT

Syntax

```
ASSERT [ [ID group [SUBKEY sub]]
         [FIELDS dobj1 dobj2 ...]
         CONDITION ] log_exp.
```

Release

6.20

Effect

Defines an assertion. If the logical expression *log_exp* is wrong (see log_exp entry), the program either cancels due to a runtime error, or the ABAP Debugger is launched, or a log entry is created.

Additions

- ID group
  Assigns the assertion to a checkpoint group group which controls its activation and behavior.
- SUBKEY sub
  Controls the aggregation of the log via subkey sub.
- FIELDS dobj1 dobj2 ...
  Writes the contents of data objects dobj1 dobj2 ... into the log or the short dump.
- CONDITION
  Must be specified before log_exp, if one of the other additions is used.

ASSIGN

Syntax

```
ASSIGN { dobj[+off][(len)]
       | [TABLE FIELD] (name)
       | oref->(attr_name)
       | {class|(class_name)}=>{attr|(attr_name)}
       | dref->*
       | {dobj INCREMENT inc}
       | {COMPONENT comp OF STRUCTURE struc} }
  TO <fs>
  [ { CASTING [ {TYPE type|(name)}
              | {LIKE dobj}
              | {[TYPE p] DECIMALS dec}
              | {TYPE HANDLE handle} ] }
  | { {TYPE name}
    | {[TYPE name] DECIMALS dec} } ]
  [RANGE range].
```

Effect

Assigns a memory area to a field symbol <fs>.

Additions

- `dobj[+off][(len)]`
  Memory area of data object `dobj` or of its sub-area `off(len)`.
- `(name)`
  Memory area of the data object contained in `name`.
- `dref->*`
  Memory area of the dereferenced reference variable `dref`.
- `COMPONENT comp OF STRUCTURE struc`
  Memory area of the component `comp` of a structure `struc`.
- `CASTING`
  Casts the memory area to the typing of the field symbol.
- `CASTING TYPE type|(name)`
  Casts the memory area to data type `type` which can also be specified as content of `name`.
- `CASTING LIKE dobj`
  Casts the memory area to the data type of data object `dobj`.
- `CASTING [TYPE p] DECIMALS dec`
  Casts the memory area to data type `p` with fractional portions specified in `dec`.

Additions since Release 6.10

- `oref->(attr_name)`
  Memory area of the attribute specified in `attr_name`, which is referenced by `oref`.
- `{class|(class_name)}=>{attr|(attr_name)}`
  Memory area of the static attribute `attr` of a class `class`, where attribute and class can be specified as contents of `attr_name` and `class_name`.
- `dobj INCREMENT inc`
  Memory area that is offset `inc` times the length of `dobj`.
- `RANGE range`
  Limits the adressable memory area to the data object `range`.

Addition since Release 6.40

- `CASTING TYPE HANDLE handle`
  Casts the memory area to the data type which is described by the type object of the RTTS that is referenced by `handle`.

Obsolete Additions

- `TABLE FIELD`
  Limits the search for the data object in `name` to interface work areas declared with `TABLES`.
- `[TYPE name] DECIMALS dec`
  Casts the memory area to an elementary ABAP type in `name` or to the fractional portions in `dec`.

ASSIGN—LOCAL COPY

Syntax

```
ASSIGN LOCAL COPY
  OF { {[INITIAL] { dobj[+off][(len)]
                  | (name)
                  | oref->(attr_name)
                  | {class|(class_name)}=>{attr|(attr_name)}
                  | dref->* } }
     | {INITIAL LINE OF {itab|(itab_name)}} }
  TO <fs>
  [CASTING ...].
```

Release

Obsolete

Effect

Creates a local anonymous data object as a copy of a memory area in a procedure, and assigns it to the field symbol <fs>.

Additions

- `LINE OF`
  The memory area is a copy of a line of an internal table.
- `INITIAL`
  Initializes the anonymous data object. Otherwise, the content of the memory area is used.
- For the other additions, see `ASSIGN`.

AT

Syntax

```
[AT FIRST.
   ...
ENDAT.]
  [AT field_groupi [WITH field_groupj].
    ...
  ENDAT.]
    [AT NEW comp1.
       ...
     ENDAT.
       ...
         [AT NEW comp2.
             ...
         ENDAT.
           [...]]]
             [ ... ]
         [[[...]
         AT END OF comp2.
             ...
           ENDAT.]
       ...
     AT END OF comp1.
       ...
     ENDAT.]
[AT LAST.
   ...
ENDAT].
```

Effect

Control level processing within `LOOP` loops over internal tables or over the extract dataset of the program, in which statement blocks that are enclosed by `AT` and `ENDAT` are executed depending on conditions that are expressed in the additions.

Additions

- `FIRST`
  First line of the internal table or the extract dataset.
- `field_groupi`
  Line of the extract dataset that was appended using the `EXTRACT field_groupi` statement.
- `WITH field_groupj`
  Condition that the next line was appended using `EXTRACT field_groupj`.
- `NEW comp1, NEW comp2, ...`
  First line of a group with identical contents in the components `comp1 comp2 ...` and in the components to the left of `comp1 comp2 ...`
- `END OF comp1, END OF comp2, ...`
  Last line of a group with identical contents in the components `comp1 comp2 ...` and in the components to the left of `comp1 comp2 ...`
- `LAST`
  Last line of the internal table or the extract dataset.

AT LINE-SELECTION

Syntax

```
AT LINE-SELECTION.
```

Effect

Initiates an event block whose event is triggered by selecting a list line using the predefined function code »PICK«.

AT PF

Syntax

```
AT PFnn.
```

Release
Obsolete

Effect
Initiates an event block whose event is selected during a list display by selecting a function using function code »PFnn«, where nn stands for a number between 01 and 24.

AT SELECTION-SCREEN

Syntax

```
AT SELECTION-SCREEN [ OUTPUT
                    | {ON {par|selcrit}}
                    | {ON END OF selcrit}
                    | {ON BLOCK block}
                    | {ON RADIOBUTTON GROUP radi}
                    | {ON {HELP-REQUEST|VALUE-REQUEST}
                       FOR {par|selcrit-low|selcrit-high}}
                    | {ON EXIT-COMMAND} ].
```

Effect
Initiates event blocks whose events are triggered at certain times during selection screen processing. If no addition is used, the event is triggered upon completion of the selection screen processing.

Additions

- `OUTPUT`
  PBO event of the selection screen.
- `ON {par|selcrit}`
  Transfer of individual parameters `par` or single fields of selection criteria `selcrit`.
- `ON END OF selcrit`
  Transfer of a selection table `selcrit`.
- `ON BLOCK block`
  Transfer of a block `block`.
- `ON RADIOBUTTON GROUP radi`
  Transfer of a radio button group `radi`.
- `ON {HELP-REQUEST|VALUE-REQUEST}`
  `FOR {par|selcrit-low|selcrit-high}`
  Requests the field help or the input help (F1, F4) for the input fields of parameters `par` or selection criteria `selcrit`.

▶ `ON EXIT-COMMAND`
Cancels the selection screen processing.

AT USER-COMMAND

Syntax

```
AT USER-COMMAND.
```

Effect

Initiates an event block whose event is triggered by a function with a self-defined function code on a list.

AUTHORITY-CHECK

Syntax

```
AUTHORITY-CHECK OBJECT auth_obj [FOR USER user]
                         ID id1  {FIELD val1}|DUMMY
                        [ID id2  {FIELD val2}|DUMMY]
                         ...
                        [ID id10 {FIELD val10}|DUMMY].
```

Effect

Performs an authorization check against the authorization object `auth_obj` for the current user or a specified user. Either the entries in the user master record are evaluated for the authorization fields `id1 ... id10` using `FIELD` or the check is skipped using `DUMMY`.

Additions

▶ `FIELD val1 ... FIELD val10`
Compares the contents of `val1 ... val10` with the values for authorization fields `id1 ... id10` in the user master record.

▶ `DUMMY`
Skips the check for authorization fields `id1 ... id10`.

Addition since Release 7.0

▶ `FOR USER user`
Checks the user specified in `user`.

BACK

Syntax

```
BACK.
```

Effect

Places the list cursor on the first position of a line block defined with RESERVE, of a page header defined behind TOP-OF-PAGE or on the first position of the first line underneath the standard page header.

BREAK-POINT

Syntax

```
BREAK-POINT [ {ID group} | {log_text} ].
```

Effect

Defines a breakpoint for branching to the ABAP Debugger.

Addition

- log_text
  Specifies a text to complement the system log.

Addition since Release 6.20

- ID group
  Assigns the breakpoint to a checkpoint group group which controls its activation. Without this addition, a breakpoint is always activated.

CALL BADI

Syntax

```
CALL BADI badi->meth    [EXPORTING  p1 = a1 p2 = a2 ...]
                      { {[IMPORTING  p1 = a1 p2 = a2 ...]
                         [CHANGING   p1 = a1 p2 = a2 ...]}
                      |  [RECEIVING   r = a  ] }
                         [EXCEPTIONS [exc1 = n1 exc2 = n2 ...]
                                     [OTHERS = n_o]].
```

Release

7.0

Effect

Calls the BAdI (Business Add-In) method meth in the object plug-ins that are referenced by the BAdI object that is referenced by the BAdI reference variable badi.

Additions

- EXPORTING p1 = a1 p2 = a2 ...
  Assigns actual parameters a1 a2 ... to input parameters p1 p2 ...
- IMPORTING p1 = a1 p2 = a2 ...
  Assigns output parameters p1 p2 ... to actual parameters a1 a2 ...
- CHANGING p1 = a1 p2 = a2 ...
  Assigns actual parameters a1 a2 ... to input/output parameters p1 p2 ...
- RECEIVING r = a
  Assigns the return value r to the actual parameter a.
- EXCEPTIONS
  Enables the handling of non-class-based exceptions:
  - exc1 = n1 exc2 = n2—Assigns numbers n1 n2 ... for the return value sy-subrc to the classical exceptions exc1 exc2 ...
  - OTHERS = n_o—Assigns a number n_o for the return value sy-subrc to all exceptions not explicitly named.

CALL CUSTOMER-FUNCTION

Syntax

```
CALL CUSTOMER-FUNCTION func
     [EXPORTING  p1 = a1 p2 = a2 ...]
     [IMPORTING  p1 = a1 p2 = a2 ...]
     [CHANGING   p1 = a1 p2 = a2 ...]
     [TABLES     t1 = itab1 t2 = itab2 ...]
     [EXCEPTIONS [exc1 = n1 exc2 = n2 ...]
                 [error_message = n_error]
                 [OTHERS = n_o]].
```

Release

Obsolete

Effect

Integrates the function module exit specified in func.

C

Additions

- EXPORTING p1 = a1 p2 = a2 ...
  Assigns actual parameters a1 a2 ... to input parameters p1 p2 ...
- IMPORTING p1 = a1 p2 = a2 ...
  Assigns output parameters p1 p2 ... to actual parameters a1 a2 ...
- CHANGING p1 = a1 p2 = a2 ...
  Assigns actual parameters a1 a2 ... to input/output parameters p1 p2 ...
- TABLES t1 = itab1 t2 = itab2 ...
  Assigns internal tables itab1 itab2 ... to table parameters t1 t2 ...
- EXCEPTIONS
  Enables the handling of non-class-based exceptions:
  - exc1 = n1 exc2 = n2—Assigns numbers n1 n2 ... for the return value sy-subrc to the classical exceptions exc1 exc2 ...
  - error_message = n_error—Handles messages via the special exception error_message.
  - OTHERS = n_o—Assigns a number n_o for the return value sy-subrc to all exceptions not explicitly named.

CALL DIALOG

Syntax

```
CALL DIALOG dialog [ {AND SKIP FIRST SCREEN}
                   | {USING bdc_tab [MODE mode]} ]
                   [ EXPORTING p1 FROM a1 p2 FROM a2 ...]
                   [ IMPORTING p1 TO a1 p2 TO a2 ...].
```

Release

Obsolete

Effect

Calls the dialog module specified in dialog.

Additions

- `AND SKIP FIRST SCREEN`
  Suspends the display of the initial screen.
- `USING bdc_tab [MODE mode]`
  Executes the dialog module via a batch input session that is defined in the internal table `bdc_tab`; a processing mode can be specified in `mode`.
- `EXPORTING p1 FROM a1 p2 FROM a2 ...`
  Assigns actual parameters `a1 a2 ...` to input parameters `p1 p2 ...`
- `IMPORTING p1 TO a1 p2 TO a2 ...`
  Assigns output parameters `p1 p2 ...` to actual parameters `a1 a2 ...`

CALL FUNCTION

Syntax

```
CALL FUNCTION func [ {IN UPDATE TASK}
                   | { [ {STARTING NEW TASK task}
                       | {IN BACKGROUND TASK} ]
                       [DESTINATION dest] }
                   | {IN BACKGROUND UNIT} ]
                   { [EXPORTING  p1 = a1 p2 = a2 ...]
                     [IMPORTING  p1 = a1 p2 = a2 ...]
                     [CHANGING   p1 = a1 p2 = a2 ...]
                     [TABLES     t1 = itab1 t2 = itab2 ...]
                     [EXCEPTIONS [exc1 = n1 exc2 = n2 ...]
                                 [error_message = n_error]
                                 [system_failure = ns
                                    [MESSAGE smess]]
                                 [communication_failure = nc
                                    [MESSAGE cmess]]
                                 [OTHERS = n_o]] }
                   | { [PARAMETER-TABLE ptab]
                       [EXCEPTION-TABLE etab] }
                   [ {PERFORMING subr}
                   | {CALLING meth} ON END OF TASK ].
```

Effect

Calls the function module specified in `func`.

Additions

- IN UPDATE TASK
  Registers an update function module.
- DESTINATION, STARTING NEW TASK, IN BACKGROUND TASK
  Synchronous, asynchronous, or transactional RFC.
- EXPORTING p1 = a1 p2 = a2 ...
  Assigns actual parameters a1 a2 ... to input parameters p1 p2 ...
- IMPORTING p1 = a1 p2 = a2 ...
  Assigns output parameters p1 p2 ... to actual parameters a1 a2 ...
- CHANGING p1 = a1 p2 = a2 ...
  Assigns actual parameters a1 a2 ... to input/output parameters p1 p2 ...
- TABLES t1 = itab1 t2 = itab2 ...
  Assigns internal tables itab1 itab2 ... to table parameters t1 t2 ...
- EXCEPTIONS
  Enables the handling of non-class-based exceptions:
  - exc1 = n1 exc2 = n2—Assigns numbers n1 n2 ... for the return value sy-subrc to the classical exceptions exc1 exc2 ...
  - error_message = n_error—Handles messages via the special exception error_message.
  - system_failure, communication_failure—Handles special RFC exceptions and adopts the first line of the short dump after smess or cmess.
  - OTHERS = n_o—Assigns a number n_o for the return value sy-subrc to all exceptions not explicitly named.
- PERFORMING subr ON END OF TASK
  Calls the subroutine subr upon completion of an asynchronous RFC.

Additions since Release 6.10

- PARAMETER-TABLE ptab
  Assigns dynamic actual parameters from an internal table ptab of the ABAP_FUNC_PARMBIND_TAB type to the formal parameters.
- EXCEPTION-TABLE etab
  Assigns dynamic return values from an internal table etab of the ABAP_FUNC_EXCPBIND_TAB type to non-class-based exceptions.

Addition since Release 6.20

- `CALLING meth ON END OF TASK`
  Calls the method `meth` upon completion of an asynchronous RFC.

Addition since Release 7.0

- `IN BACKGROUND UNIT unit`
  Transactional RFC with context object referenced by the reference variable `unit`.

CALL METHOD

Syntax forms

Static form

```
[CALL METHOD]
{meth
|oref->meth
|super->meth
|class=>meth}( { }
             | { a }
             | p1 = a1 p2 = a2 ...
             | {  [EXPORTING p1 = a1 p2 = a2 ...]
                {{[IMPORTING p1 = a1 p2 = a2 ...]
                  [CHANGING  p1 = a1 p2 = a2 ...]}
                | [RECEIVING r  = a ]}
                  [EXCEPTIONS [exc1 = n1
                               exc2 = n2 ...]
                              [OTHERS = n_o]] } ).
```

Dynamic form

```
CALL METHOD {(meth_name)
            |oref->(meth_name)
            |(class_name)=>(meth_name)
            |class=>(meth_name)
            |(class_name)=>meth} [PARAMETER-TABLE ptab]
                                 [EXCEPTION-TABLE etab].
```

Effect

Calls a method. To some extent, static additions also can be used in the dynamic form.

Additions

- `meth`
  Specifies the `meth` method of the same class.
- `oref->meth`
  Specifies the instance method `meth` of the object referenced by `oref`.
- `super->meth`
  Specifies the `meth` method in the direct superclass.
- `class=>meth`
  Specifies the static method `meth` of the class `class`.
- `(meth_name)`
  Specifies the method contained in `meth_name`.
- `(class_name)`
  Specifies the class contained in `class_name`.
- `( )`
  Short form for calling a method without passing on any parameter.
- `( a )`
  Short form for calling a method and passing on a single parameter `a`.
- `( p1 = a1 p2 = a2 ... )`
  Short form for calling a method and passing on multiple parameters `a1`, `a2`, ...
- `EXPORTING p1 = a1 p2 = a2 ...`
  Assigns actual parameters `a1 a2 ...` to input parameters `p1 p2 ...`
- `IMPORTING p1 = a1 p2 = a2 ...`
  Assigns output parameters `p1 p2 ...` to actual parameters `a1 a2 ...`
- `CHANGING p1 = a1 p2 = a2 ...`
  Assigns actual parameters `a1 a2 ...` to input/output parameters `p1 p2 ...`
- `RECEIVING r = a`
  Assigns the return value `r` to the actual parameter `a`.
- `EXCEPTIONS`
  Enables the handling of non-class-based exceptions:
  - `exc1 = n1 exc2 = n2`—Assigns numbers `n1 n2 ...` for the return value `sy-subrc` to the classical exceptions `exc1 exc2 ...`

– OTHERS = n_o—Assigns a number n_o for the return value sy-subrc to all exceptions not explicitly named.

- PARAMETER-TABLE ptab
  Assigns dynamic actual parameters from an internal table ptab of the ABAP_ PARMBIND_TAB type to the formal parameters.
- EXCEPTION-TABLE etab
  Assigns dynamic return values from an internal table etab of the ABAP_EXCPBIND_TAB type to non-class-based exceptions.

Addition since Release 6.10

- (...)
  In the static form, all variants of the parameters list can be listed in parenthesis, and with parenthetical parameter lists you don't need to add CALL METHOD.

CALL METHOD—OLE

Syntax

```
CALL METHOD OF ole meth [= rc]
               [EXPORTING p1 = f1 p2 = f2 ...]
               [NO FLUSH] [QUEUE-ONLY].
```

Effect

Calls a method meth of an automation object created with CREATE OBJECT ole; the return value can be stored in a variable rc.

Additions

- EXPORTING p1 = f1 p2 = f2 ...
  Assigns actual parameters f1 f2 ... to input parameters p1 p2 ...
- NO FLUSH
  Defines that the method call isn't passed on to the presentation layer until the function module FLUSH is called or the screen is changed.
- QUEUE-ONLY
  Defines that during a flush the return values of the automation queue methods called with CALL METHOD OF are not written to the data objects rc.

C

CALL SCREEN

Syntax

```
CALL SCREEN dynnr
            [STARTING AT col1 lin1
            [ENDING   AT col2 lin2]].
```

Effect

Calls the dynpro of the number specified in dynnr and starts a dynpro sequence that is defined by the following dynpros of the dynpro that has been called.

Additions

- STARTING AT col1 lin1
  Opens a modal dialog box at the position specified in col1 and lin1.
- ENDING AT col2 lin2
  Determines that the lower right-hand corner of the modal dialog box is at the position specified in col2 and lin2.

CALL SELECTION-SCREEN

Syntax

```
CALL SELECTION-SCREEN dynnr
                      [STARTING AT col1 lin1
                      [ENDING   AT col2 lin2]]
                      [USING SELECTION-SET variant].
```

Effect

Calls the selection screen of the number specified in dynnr and starts the selection screen processing.

Additions

- STARTING AT col1 lin1
  Opens a modal dialog box at the position specified in col1 and lin1.
- ENDING AT col2 lin2
  Determines that the lower right-hand corner of the modal dialog box is at the position specified in col2 and lin2.
- USING SELECTION-SET variant
  Specifies a variant from which the default values are taken.

CALL TRANSACTION

Syntax

```
CALL TRANSACTION ta { [AND SKIP FIRST SCREEN]
                    | [USING bdc_tab
                             {{[MODE mode]
                               [UPDATE upd]}
                              |[OPTIONS FROM opt]}
                             [MESSAGES INTO itab] ] }.
```

Effect

Calls the transaction of the transaction code specified in ta and returns to the calling point.

Additions

- AND SKIP FIRST SCREEN
  Suspends the display of the initial screen.
- USING bdc_tab
  Executes the transaction via a batch input session that is defined in the internal table bdc_tab.
  - In mode following MODE, you can specify the processing mode for the batch input processing.
  - In upd following UPDATE, you can specify the update mode for the batch input processing.
  - In opt following OPTIONS FROM,you can specify the processing and update modes of the batch input processing.
  - In internal table itab following MESSAGES INTO, the messages of the batch input processing are collected.

CALL TRANSFORMATION

Syntax

```
CALL TRANSFORMATION {trans|(name)}
                     [PARAMETERS {p1 = e1 p2 = e2 ...}|(ptab)]
                     [OBJECTS    {o1 = e1 o2 = e2 ...}|(otab)]
                     [OPTIONS    {a1 = e1 a2 = e2 ...}]
     SOURCE {XML sxml}
          | {{bn1 = e1 bn2 = e2 ...}|(stab)}
     RESULT {XML rxml}
          | {{bn1 = f1 bn2 = f2 ...}|(rtab)}.
```

Release
6.10

Effect
Calls an XSL transformation or a simple transformation statically specified in `trans` or dynamically specified in `name` (since Release 6.40, see pages 195–212). Calling the predefined transformation "ID" serializes or deserializes ABAP data into the XML format or out of it respectively (ABAP Serialization XML).

Additions

- `PARAMETERS {p1 = e1 p2 = e2 ...}|ptab`
  Passes on parameters specified either individually as `p1 = e1 p2 = e2 ...` or in an internal table `ptab` to the transformation. Since Release 6.20, this is also possible for object references.

- `SOURCE XML sxml`
  Specifies an XML document in `sxml` as the source to be transformed.

- `RESULT {XML rxml}|{{bn1 = f1 bn2 = f2 ...}|(rtab)}`
  Specifies the storage of the transformation result. Either an XML document in `rxml` or data objects specified individually as `bn1 = f1 bn2 = f2 ...` or in an internal table `rtab`.

Addition since Release 6.20

- `SOURCE {bn1 = e1 bn2 = e2 ...}|(stab)`
  Specifies data objects that are listed individually as `bn1 = e1 bn2 = e2 ...` or in an internal table `stab` as the source to be transformed.

Addition since Release 6.4

- `OPTIONS {a1 = e1 a2 = e2 ...}`
  Passes control parameters on to the transformation.

Obsolete addition

- `OBJECTS {o1 = e1 o2 = e2 ...}|otab`
  Passes object references specified individually as `o1 = e1 o2 = e2 ...` or in an internal table `otab` on to the transformation (obsolete since Release 6.20).

CASE

Syntax

```
CASE operand.
  [WHEN operand1 [OR operand2 [OR operand3 [...]]].
```

```
    [statement_block1]]
   ...
   [WHEN OTHERS.
     [statement_blockn]]
ENDCASE.
```

Effect

Defines a control structure with multiple statement blocks statement_block1 ... statement_blockn. The first statement block in which the content of the operand operand in the WHEN statement corresponds to the content of one of the operands operand1 operand2 ... is executed. If no agreement is found, the statement block after the WHEN OTHERS statement is executed.

CATCH SYSTEM-EXCEPTIONS

Syntax

```
CATCH SYSTEM-EXCEPTIONS [exc1 = n1 exc2 = n2 ...]
                        [OTHERS = n_o].
  [statement_block]
ENDCATCH.
```

Release

Obsolete

Effect

Catches catchable runtime errors that appear in the statement block statement_block. The catchable runtime errors are either specified individually or as exception groups exc1 exc2 ... If one of the specified runtime errors occurs, the respective number n1 n2 ... is assigned to the system field sy-subrc and the program execution is continued after the ENDCATCH statement. The OTHERS statement catches all catchable runtime errors.

CHECK

Syntax

```
CHECK log_exp|SELECT-OPTIONS.
```

Release

Obsolete outside loops since 6.10.

Effect

Leaves a loop or a processing block if the logical expression *log_exp* (see log_exp entry) is wrong. Within a loop, the current loop pass is left and the subsequent loop pass is executed. Outside a loop, the current processing block exits.

Addition

- SELECT-OPTIONS
  Leaves GET event blocks due to selection tables.

CLASS

Syntax forms

Declaration Part

```
CLASS class DEFINITION [INHERITING FROM superclass]
                       [ABSTRACT]
                       [FINAL]
                       [CREATE {PUBLIC|PROTECTED|PRIVATE}]
                       [SHARED MEMORY ENABLED]
                       [FOR TESTING]
                       [[GLOBAL] FRIENDS [class1 class2 ...]
                                         [intf1 intf2 ...] ].
  [PUBLIC SECTION.
    [components]]
  [PRCTECTED SECTION.
    [components]]
  [PRIVATE SECTION.
    [components]]
ENDCLASS.
```

Implementation Part

```
CLASS class IMPLEMENTATION.
  implementations
ENDCLASS.
```

Effect

Declaration and implementation of a class class. In the declaration part the components components of a class are declared with ALIASES, [CLASS-]DATA, [CLASS-]METHODS and [CLASS-]EVENTS in the visibility areas PUBLIC, PROTECTED and PRIVATE SECTION. In the implementation part, all concrete methods declared in the declaration part are implemented between METHOD and ENDMETHOD.

Additions

- INHERITING FROM superclass
  Defines class as a subclass of superclass.
- ABSTRACT
  Defines class as an abstract class that cannot be instantiated.
- FINAL
  Defines class as a final class from which no subclasses can be derived.
- CREATE {PUBLIC|PROTECTED|PRIVATE}
  Determines that the class class can be instantiated as public, protected, or private.

Addition since Release 6.10

- [GLOBAL] FRIENDS [class1 class2 ...] [intf1 intf2 ...]
  Declares other classes class1 class2 ... or interfaces intf1 intf2 ... as friends that are permitted to access protected and private components of class.

Additions since Release 6.40

- SHARED MEMORY ENABLED
  Specifies that instances of the class can be stored in shared memory.
- FOR TESTING
  Defines a test class for ABAP Unit.

CLASS—DEFERRED, LOAD

Syntax

```
CLASS class DEFINITION {DEFERRED [PUBLIC]} | LOAD.
```

Effect

Announces a class.

Additions

- DEFERRED [PUBLIC]
  Deferred declaration of a local or global class before its actual declaration in the program.
- LOAD
  Loads a global class from the class library.

CLASS-DATA

Syntax

```
CLASS-DATA attr[(len)] [TYPE { {abap_type [LENGTH len]
                                          [DECIMALS dec]}
                             | {[LINE OF] type}
                             | {REF TO type}
                             | { {{[STANDARD] TABLE}
                                 |{SORTED TABLE}
                                 |{HASHED TABLE}}
                                 OF [REF TO] type
                                 [WITH [UNIQUE|NON-UNIQUE]
                                       {KEY comp1 comp2 ...}
                                      |{DEFAULT KEY}]
                                 [INITIAL SIZE n]}
                               | {RANGE OF type
                                    [INITIAL SIZE n]} }]
                       | [LIKE { {[LINE OF] dobj}
                             | {REF TO dobj}
                             | { {{[STANDARD] TABLE}
                                 |{SORTED TABLE}
                                 |{HASHED TABLE}}
                                 OF [REF TO] dobj
                                 [WITH [UNIQUE|NON-UNIQUE]
                                       {KEY comp1 comp2 ...}
                                      |{DEFAULT KEY}]
                                 [INITIAL SIZE n]}
                               | {RANGE OF dobj
                                    [INITIAL SIZE n]} }]
                         [VALUE { val | {IS INITIAL} }]
                         [READ-ONLY].
```

Effect

Declares a static attribute `attr` of a class or an interface.

Additions

- `(len)`
  Determines the length when referring to generic built-in ABAP types.
- `TYPE`
  Determines the type by referring to a data type.

- `LIKE`
  Determines the type by referring to a data object.
- `DECIMALS dec`
  Determines the number of fractional portions when referring to generic built-in ABAP type `p`.
- `LINE OF`
  Determines the type by referring to the line type of an internal table.
- `REF TO`
  Creates a reference variable.
- `{[STANDARD] TABLE}|{SORTED TABLE}|{HASHED TABLE}`
  Creates a standard, sorted or hashed table.
- `WITH {[UNIQUE|NON-UNIQUE] {KEY comp1 comp2 ...}}|{DEFAULT KEY}`
  Defines a unique or non-unique table key. The components of the key are either specified explicitly or defined by a standard key.
- `INITIAL SIZE n`
  Defines the initial memory allocation for an internal table.
- `RANGE OF`
  Defines a ranges table with the line type of a selection table.
- `VALUE { val | {IS INITIAL} }`
  Sets the start value of the attribute to `val` or to the initial value.
- `READ-ONLY`
  Protects public attributes against write accesses from outside their own class.

Additions since Release 6.10

- `LENGTH len`
  Determines the length when referring to generic built-in ABAP types.

CLASS-EVENTS

Syntax

```
CLASS-EVENTS evt [ EXPORTING VALUE(p1) typing
                               [OPTIONAL|{DEFAULT def1}]
                             VALUE(p2) typing
                               [OPTIONAL|{DEFAULT def2}]
                             ... ].
```

Effect

Declares a static event evt of a class or an interface.

Additions

- EXPORTING VALUE(p1) ... VALUE(p2) ...
  Defines the output parameters p1 p2 ... of the event.
- *typing*
  Types the output parameters. See typing entry.
- OPTIONAL|DEFAULT
  Determines optional output parameters either with or without default parameters def1 def2 ...

CLASS-METHODS

Syntax

```
CLASS-METHODS meth [FOR EVENT evt OF {class|intf}]
  [ IMPORTING {{VALUE(p1)|REFERENCE(p1)|p1} typing
                  [OPTIONAL|DEFAULT def1]
               {VALUE(p2)|REFERENCE(p2)|p2} typing
                   [OPTIONAL|DEFAULT def2]
               ... }
              [PREFERRED PARAMETER p] ]
  [ EXPORTING {{VALUE(p1)|REFERENCE(p1)|p1} typing
               {VALUE(p2)|REFERENCE(p2)|p2} typing
              ... } ]
  [ CHANGING  {{VALUE(p1)|REFERENCE(p1)|p1} typing
                  [OPTIONAL|DEFAULT def1]
               {VALUE(p2)|REFERENCE(p2)|p2} typing
                  [OPTIONAL|DEFAULT def2]
              ... } ]
  [ RETURNING {VALUE(r)} typing ]
  [ {RAISING|EXCEPTIONS} exc1 exc2 ... ].
```

Effect

Declares a static method meth of a class or an interface.

Additions

- FOR EVENT evt OF {class|intf}
  Declares an event-handler method that can deal with the event evt of the class class or of the interface intf. Only input parameters are possible.

- `IMPORTING`
  Defines input parameters `p1 p2 ...`
- `EXPORTING`
  Defines output parameters `p1 p2 ...`
- `CHANGING`
  Defines input/output parameters `p1 p2 ...`
- `RETURNING`
  Declares a functional method with a completely typed return value `r`.
- `VALUE(p1) VALUE(p2) ...`
  Defines pass by value for a formal parameter.
- `REFERENCE(p1) REFERENCE(p2) ... | p1 p2 ...`
  Defines pass by reference for a formal parameter.
- *`typing`*
  Types the formal parameters. See `typing` entry.
- `OPTIONAL|DEFAULT`
  Determines optional input or output parameters either without or with default parameters `def1 def2 ...`
- `PREFERRED PARAMETER p`
  Declares a parameter `p` out of exclusively optional input parameters as a preferred parameter.

Addition since Release 6.10

- `RAISING exc1 exc2 ...`
  Declares class-based exceptions `exc1 exc2 ...` that can be propagated from the method.

Obsolete addition

- `EXCEPTIONS exc1 exc2 ...`
  Defines non-class-based exceptions `exc1 exc2 ...`

CLASS-POOL

Syntax

```
CLASS-POOL [MESSAGE-ID mid].
```

Effect

Initiates a class pool.

Addition

- `MESSAGE-ID mid`
  Determines a message class `mid` for short forms of `MESSAGE`.

CLEAR

Syntax

```
CLEAR dobj [ {WITH val [IN {BYTE|CHARACTER} MODE]}
           | {WITH NULL} ].
```

Effect

Initializes a data object dobj by assigning the type-specific initial value.

Addition

- WITH val
  Fills the data object with the byte or character specified in val.

Addition since Release 6.10

- IN {BYTE|CHARACTER} MODE
  Determines byte or character string processing.

Obsolete addition

- WITH NULL
  Replaces all bytes in dobj with the hexadecimal 0 value.

CLOSE CURSOR

Syntax

```
CLOSE CURSOR dbcur.
```

Effect

Closes a database cursor linked to dbcur that was previously opened with the OPEN CURSOR statement.

CLOSE DATASET

Syntax

```
CLOSE DATASET dset.
```

Effect

Closes a file specified in dset on the application server that was previously opened with the OPEN DATASET statement.

COLLECT

Syntax

```
COLLECT wa INTO itab { [ASSIGNING <fs> [CASTING]]
                     | [REFERENCE INTO dref] }.
```

Effect

Inserts a work area wa as a line into an internal table itab, where, for a line whose table key already exists, the values of other components are added to those of the existing line.

Additions since Release 6.10

- ASSIGNING <fs>
  Assigns the inserted line to the field symbol <fs>.
- REFERENCE INTO dref
  Sets the data reference in dref to the inserted line.

Addition since Release 7.0

- CASTING
  Casts the line to the typing of the field symbol.

COMMIT

Syntax

```
COMMIT WORK [AND WAIT].
```

Effect

Terminates an SAP LUW. The subroutines registered with PERFORM ON COMMIT and update function modules registered with CALL FUNCTION IN UPDATE TASK are executed.

Addition

- AND WAIT
  The current program waits until all high-priority update function modules have been executed.

COMMUNICATION

Syntax

```
COMMUNICATION { {INIT DESTINATION dest}
              | {ALLOCATE}
              | {ACCEPT}
```

```
| {SEND BUFFER buf}
| {RECEIVE BUFFER buf
           DATAINFO dat
           STATUSINFO stat}
| {DEALLOCATE} } ID id
[RETURNCODE rc]
[LENGTH leng]
[RECEIVED rec]
[HOLD].
```

C

Release

Obsolete

Effect

Carries out a communication with external programs via the CPI-C interface whose connection number is specified in `id`.

Additions

- `INIT DESTINATION dest`
  Initializes a connection `dest`.
- `ALLOCATE`
  Establishes a connection.
- `ACCEPT`
  Accepts a connection.
- `SEND BUFFER buf`
  Sends data in `buf`.
- `RECEIVE BUFFER buf DATAINFO dat STATUSINFO stat`
  Receives data in `buf` and status information in `dat` and `stat`.
- `DEALLOCATE`
  De-establishes a connection.
- `RETURNCODE rc`
  Receives a return value in `rc`.
- `LENGTH leng`
  Limits the length of data sent or received to `leng`.
- `RECEIVED rec`
  Returns the amount of bytes received in `rec`.
- `HOLD`
  Prevents changing of the internal session during the reception process.

COMPUTE

Syntax

```
[COMPUTE]
result = { [+|-] operand1
           [{+|-|*|/|DIV|MOD|**} [+|-] operand2
           [{+|-|*|/|DIV|MOD|**} [+|-] operand3
           ... ]] }
       | { [BIT-NOT] operand1
           [{BIT-AND|BIT-OR|BIT-XOR} [BIT-NOT] operand2
           [{BIT-AND|BIT-OR|BIT-XOR} [BIT-NOT] operand3
           ...  ]] }.
```

Effect

Calculates an arithmetic expression that consists of algebraic signs (+, -), operands `operand1 operand2 ...` and the arithmetic operators +, -, *, /, `DIV`, `MOD` and `**`, or calculates a bit expression consisting of a negation operator (`BIT-NOT`), operands `operand1 operand2 ...` and the bit operators `BIT-AND`, `BIT-OR` and `BIT-XOR`. Assigns the result `result`.

CONCATENATE

Syntax

```
CONCATENATE {dobj1 dobj2 ...}|{LINES OF itab}
            INTO result
            [IN {BYTE|CHARACTER} MODE]
            [SEPARATED BY sep]
            [RESPECTING BLANKS].
```

Effect

Concatenates the contents of `dobj1 dobj2 ...` and assigns the result to `result`.

Addition

- `SEPARATED BY sep`
  Specifies a separating byte or character in `sep`.

Addition since Release 6.10

- `IN {BYTE|CHARACTER} MODE`
  Determines byte or character string processing.

Additions since Release 7.0

- `LINES OF itab`
  Concatenates the contents of lines of an internal table `itab`.
- `RESPECTING BLANKS`
  Defines that trailing blanks are taken into account in `dobj1 dobj2 ...` or the lines of `itab` respectively.

C

CONDENSE

Syntax

```
CONDENSE text [NO-GAPS].
```

Effect

Condenses the character string in `text` by removing leading and trailing blanks and replaces multiple consecutive blanks by a single blank.

Addition

- `NO-GAPS`
  Removes all blanks from the character string.

CONSTANTS

Syntax

```
CONSTANTS const[(len)] [TYPE { {abap_type [LENGTH len]
                                          [DECIMALS dec]}
                             | {[LINE OF] type}
                             | {REF TO type}
                             | {  {{[STANDARD] TABLE}
                                  |{SORTED TABLE}
                                  |{HASHED TABLE}}
                                  OF [REF TO] type
                                  [WITH [UNIQUE|NON-UNIQUE]
                                        {KEY comp1 comp2 ...}
                                       |{DEFAULT KEY}]
                                  [INITIAL SIZE n]
                                  [WITH HEADER LINE]}
                               | {RANGE OF type
                                    [INITIAL SIZE n]
                                    [WITH HEADER LINE]} }]
                       | [LIKE { {[LINE OF] dobj}
                               | {REF TO dobj}
```

```
                    | { {{[STANDARD] TABLE}
                        |{SORTED TABLE}
                        |{HASHED TABLE}}
                        OF [REF TO] dobj
                        [WITH [UNIQUE|NON-UNIQUE]
                               {KEY comp1 comp2 ...}
                              |{DEFAULT KEY}]
                        [INITIAL SIZE n]
                        [WITH HEADER LINE]}
                      | {RANGE OF dobj
                           [INITIAL SIZE n]
                           [WITH HEADER LINE]} }]
               VALUE { val | {IS INITIAL} }.
```

Effect

Declares a constant `const`.

Additions

- `(len)`
  Determines the length when referring to generic built-in ABAP types.
- `TYPE`
  Determines the type by referring to a data type.
- `LIKE`
  Determines the type by referring to a data object.
- `DECIMALS dec`
  Determines the number of fractional portions when referring to generic built-in ABAP type `p`.
- `LINE OF`
  Determines the type by referring to the line type of an internal table.
- `REF TO`
  Creates a reference variable.
- `{[STANDARD] TABLE}|{SORTED TABLE}|{HASHED TABLE}`
  Creates a standard, sorted or hashed table.
- `WITH {[UNIQUE|NON-UNIQUE] {KEY comp1 comp2 ...}}|{DEFAULT KEY}`
  Defines a unique or non-unique table key. The components of the key are either specified explicitly or defined by a standard key.
- `INITIAL SIZE n`
  Defines the initial memory allocation for an internal table.

- RANGE OF
  Defines a ranges table with the line type of a selection table.
- VALUE { val | {IS INITIAL} }
  Sets the start value of the constant to val or to the initial value.

Addition since Release 6.10

- LENGTH len
  Determines the length when referring to generic built-in ABAP types.

Obsolete addition

- WITH HEADER LINE
  Defines a header line having the same name as const for an internal table.

CONTEXTS

Syntax

```
CONTEXTS con.
```

Release

Obsolete

Effect

Creates a structured data type context_con in order to create an instance of the context con.

CONTINUE

Syntax

```
CONTINUE.
```

Effect

Leaves a loop. The current loop pass is left, and the subsequent loop pass is executed.

CONTROLS

Syntax

```
CONTROLS contrl TYPE { TABLEVIEW USING SCREEN dynnr }
                   | { TABSTRIP }.
```

Effect

Declares the use of a control `contrl` on a dynpro of the program. A structure having the name of the control is created to manage the control.

Additions

- `TABLEVIEW USING SCREEN dynnr`
  Declares the use of a table control for the dynpro specified in `dynnr`.
- `TABSTRIP`
  Declares the use of a tabstrip control.

CONVERT DATE

Syntax

```
CONVERT {DATE dat1 INTO INVERTED-DATE dat2}
      | {INVERTED-DATE dat1 INTO DATE dat2}.
```

Release

Obsolete

Effect

Both variants convert the digits of a character-type data object `dat1` into their complement on nine and assign the result to the data object `dat2`.

CONVERT TEXT

Syntax

```
CONVERT TEXT text INTO SORTABLE CODE hex.
```

Effect

Converts a character string in `text` into a byte string that can be sorted and assigns the result to `hex`. Standard sorting of such a byte string results in a sort order in which the output fields are sorted according to the current locale.

CONVERT TIME STAMP

Syntax

```
CONVERT { TIME STAMP time_stamp TIME ZONE tz
          INTO [DATE dat] [TIME tim]
            [DAYLIGHT SAVING TIME dst] }
      | { DATE dat [TIME tim
            [DAYLIGHT SAVING TIME dst]]
          INTO TIME STAMP time_stamp TIME ZONE tz }.
```

Effect

Either converts a date in `dat` and a time and `tim` that are related to a time zone `tz` into a UTC time stamp and returns the result in `time_stamp`, or converts a UTC time stamp in `time_stamp` into date and time specifications and returns the results in `dat` and `tim`.

Addition since Release 6.20

- `DAYLIGHT SAVING TIME dst`

  For `CONVERT DATE`, determines whether the time specification refers to daylight saving time. For `CONVERT TIME STAMP`, determines whether the time stamp specification refers to daylight saving time.

CREATE DATA

Syntax

```
CREATE DATA dref [ AREA HANDLE handle ]
                 [ TYPE { {abap_type|(name)
                             [LENGTH len] [DECIMALS dec]}
                        | {[LINE OF] type|(name)}
                        | {REF TO type|(name)}
                        | {{{[STANDARD] TABLE}
                             |{SORTED TABLE}
                             |{HASHED TABLE}}
                            OF [REF TO] {type|(name)}
                            [WITH [UNIQUE|NON-UNIQUE]
                                   {KEY comp1 comp2 ...}
                                  |{DEFAULT KEY}]
                            [INITIAL SIZE n]}
                        | {HANDLE handle} } ]
               | [ LIKE { {[LINE OF] dobj}
                        | {REF TO dobj}
                        | {{{[STANDARD] TABLE}
```

```
                    |{SORTED TABLE}
                    |{HASHED TABLE}}
                    OF dobj
                    [WITH [UNIQUE|NON-UNIQUE]
                     {KEY comp1 comp2 ...}
                    |{DEFAULT KEY}]
                    [INITIAL SIZE n]} } ].
```

Effect

Creates an anonymous data object and sets the data reference in `dref` to the data object. If none of the `TYPE` or `LIKE` additions is specified, `dref` must be completely typed and this type will be used for the data object.

Additions

- `TYPE`
  Determines the type by referring to a data type.
- `LIKE`
  Determines the type by referring to a data object.
- `[LINE OF] type|(name)`
  Specifies statically or dynamically a previously defined data type in which `LINE OF` enables referencing the line type of an internal table.

Additions since Release 6.10

- `abap_type|(name) [LENGTH len] [DECIMALS dec]`
  Specifies a built-in elementary data type statically or dynamically and determines the length and number of fractional portions.
- `REF TO`
  Creates a reference variable.
- `{[STANDARD] TABLE}|{SORTED TABLE}|{HASHED TABLE}`
  Creates a standard, sorted or hashed table.
- `WITH {[UNIQUE|NON-UNIQUE] {KEY comp1 comp2 ...}}|{DEFAULT KEY}`
  Defines a unique or non-unique table key. The components of the key are either specified explicitly or defined by a standard key.
- `INITIAL SIZE n`
  Defines the initial memory allocation for an internal table.

Addition since Release 6.40

- `HANDLE handle`
  Specifies the data type via a reference `handle` to a type object of the RTTS.

Addition since Release 7.0

- `AREA HANDLE handle`
  Creates a shared object, where a reference to an area handle must be specified in `handle`.

CREATE OBJECT

Syntax

```
CREATE OBJECT oref [AREA HANDLE handle]
                   [TYPE {class|(name)}]
                   { {[EXPORTING p1 = a1 p2 = a2 ...]
                      [EXCEPTIONS exc1 = n1 exc2 = n2 ...]}
                   | {[PARAMETER-TABLE ptab]
                      [EXCEPTION-TABLE etab]} }.
```

Effect

Creates an instance of a class and sets the object reference in `oref` to the object. If the `TYPE` addition is not specified, `oref` must be typed with reference to a specific class, and this class is instantiated.

Additions

- `TYPE {class|(name)}`
  Determines statically or dynamically the class of the object, which must be more special than the static type of `oref`.

- `EXPORTING p1 = a1 p2 = a2 ...`
  Assigns actual parameters `a1 a2 ...` to input parameters `p1 p2 ...` of the instance constructor.

- `EXCEPTIONS exc1 = n1 exc2 = n2 ...`
  Assigns return values to non-class-based exceptions of the instance constructor.

Additions since Release 6.10

- `PARAMETER-TABLE ptab`
  Assigns dynamic actual parameters to the formal parameters via an internal table `ptab` of the ABAP_ PARMBIND_TAB type.

- `EXCEPTION-TABLE etab`
  Assigns dynamic return values to non-class-based exceptions via an internal table `etab` of the ABAP_ EXCPBIND_ TAB type.

Addition since Release 6.40

- AREA HANDLE handle

  Creates a shared object, where a reference to an area handle must be specified in handle.

CREATE OBJECT—OLE

Syntax

```
CREATE OBJECT ole class [NO FLUSH] [QUEUE-ONLY].
```

Effect

Creates an OLE automation object ole of the automation class class, where ole must be of the ole2_object type from the OLE2 type pool and class specifies the name of the class.

Additions

- NO FLUSH

  Defines that the request for object creation isn't passed on to the presentation server until the function module FLUSH is called or the screen is changed.

- QUEUE-ONLY

  Defines that during a flush the return values of the automation queue methods called with CALL METHOD OF are not written to the data objects rc.

DATA

Syntax

```
DATA var[(len)] [TYPE { {abap_type [LENGTH len]
                                   [DECIMALS dec]}
                      | {[LINE OF] type}
                      | {REF TO type}
                      | {  {{[STANDARD] TABLE}
                           |{SORTED TABLE}
                           |{HASHED TABLE}}
                          OF [REF TO] type
                          [WITH [UNIQUE|NON-UNIQUE]
                                {KEY comp1 comp2 ...}
                               |{DEFAULT KEY}]
                          [INITIAL SIZE n]
                          [WITH HEADER LINE]}
```

```
               | {RANGE OF type
                    [INITIAL SIZE n]
                    [WITH HEADER LINE]} }]
   | [LIKE { {[LINE OF] dobj}
           | {REF TO dobj}
           | { {{[STANDARD] TABLE}
                |{SORTED TABLE}
                |{HASHED TABLE}}
               OF [REF TO] dobj
               [WITH [UNIQUE|NON-UNIQUE]
                      {KEY comp1 comp2 ...}
                     |{DEFAULT KEY}]
               [INITIAL SIZE n]
               [WITH HEADER LINE]}
             | {RANGE OF dobj
                  [INITIAL SIZE n]
                  [WITH HEADER LINE]} }]
     [VALUE { val | {IS INITIAL} }]
     [READ-ONLY].
```

Effect

Declares a variable or an instance attribute var.

Additions

- (len)
  Determines the length when referring to generic built-in ABAP types.
- TYPE
  Determines the type by referring to a data type.
- LIKE
  Determines the type by referring to a data object.
- DECIMALS dec
  Determines the number of fractional portions when referring to generic built-in ABAP type p.
- LINE OF
  Determines the type by referring to the line type of an internal table.
- REF TO
  Creates a reference variable.

- `{[STANDARD] TABLE}|{SORTED TABLE}|{HASHED TABLE}`
  Creates a standard, sorted, or hashed table.
- `WITH {[UNIQUE|NON-UNIQUE] {KEY comp1 comp2 ...}}|{DEFAULT KEY}`
  Defines a unique or non-unique table key. The components of the key are either specified explicitly or defined by a standard key.
- `INITIAL SIZE n`
  Defines the initial memory allocation for an internal table.
- `RANGE OF`
  Defines a ranges table with the line type of a selection table.
- `VALUE { val | {IS INITIAL} }`
  Sets the start value of the data object to `val` or to the initial value.
- `READ-ONLY`
  Protects public attributes against write accesses from outside their own class.

Addition since Release 6.10

- `LENGTH len`
  Determines the length when referring to generic built-in ABAP types.

Obsolete addition

- `WITH HEADER LINE`
  Defines a header with the same name as `var` for an internal table.

DATA BEGIN OF

Syntax

```
DATA BEGIN OF struc [READ-ONLY] [OCCURS n].
  ...
  DATA | INCLUDE ...
  ...
DATA END OF struc [VALID BETWEEN intlim1 AND intlim2].
```

Effect

Declares a structured data object or instance attribute `struc`, the components of which can be declared with any `DATA` statement or included from other structures with `INCLUDE`.

Addition

- `READ-ONLY`
  Protects the structure against write accesses from outside its own class.

Obsolete Additions

- `OCCURS n`
  Creates an internal table with a structured line type, standard key, a header line and an initial memory allocation `n`.
- `VALID BETWEEN intlim1 AND intlim2`
  Defines the columns `intlim1` and `intlim2` of an internal table created using `OCCURS` as interval limits for the obsolete short form of `PROVIDE`.

D

DATA—COMMON PART

Syntax

```
DATA BEGIN OF COMMON PART [name].
  ...
  DATA ...
  ...
DATA END OF COMMON PART [name].
```

Release

Obsolete

Effect

Defines a global interface work area that can be shared by the programs of a program group.

Addition

- `name`
  Defines a name for the interface work area.

DATA—OCCURS

Syntax

```
DATA itab { {TYPE [REF TO] type}
          | {LIKE [REF TO] dobj} } OCCURS n
          [WITH HEADER LINE].
```

Release

Obsolete

Effect

Declares a standard table with a standard key and the initial memory allocation `n`.

Additions

- TYPE
  Determines the line type by referring to a data type.
- LIKE
  Determines the line type by referring to a data object.
- REF TO
  Creates the line type as reference type.
- WITH HEADER LINE
  Defines a header line having the same name as itab.

DEFINE

Syntax

```
DEFINE macro.
  ... &1 ... &9 ...
END-OF-DEFINITION.
```

Effect

Defines a macro macro that consists of ABAP statements between DEFINE and END-OF-DEFINITION and can contain placeholders &1 ... &9. The macro can be incorporated into the source code after its definition by specifying its name.

DELETE DATASET

Syntax

```
DELETE DATASET dset.
```

Effect

Deletes the file specified in dset on the application server.

DELETE dbtab

Syntax

```
DELETE { {FROM {dbtab|(dbtab_syntax)} [CLIENT SPECIFIED]
         [WHERE sql_cond]}
       | {{dbtab|(dbtab_syntax)} [CLIENT SPECIFIED]
        FROM { wa|{TABLE itab} } } }.
```

Effect

Deletes rows from a database table.

Additions

- `FROM {dbtab|(dbtab_syntax)}`
  Specifies the database table statically or dynamically.
- `CLIENT SPECIFIED`
  Switches off the automatic client handling.
- `WHERE sql_cond`
  Specifies the rows to be deleted by a condition *sql_cond* (see `sql_cond` entry).
- `FROM { wa|{TABLE itab} }`
  Specifies the rows to be deleted by corresponding to the key values of a work area `wa` or to the lines of an internal table `itab`.

Additions since Release 6.10

- `(dbtab_syntax)`
  In addition to flat character-type fields, strings and internal tables with a character-type line type can also be specified.
- `[WHERE sql_cond]`
  The use of the `WHERE` condition is optional.

DELETE itab

Syntax

```
DELETE { { {TABLE itab
             {{FROM wa}
             |{WITH TABLE KEY comp_name1|(name1) = dobj1
                              comp_name2|(name2) = dobj2
                              ... }}}
         | {itab INDEX idx} }
       | {itab [FROM idx1] [TO idx2] [WHERE log_exp]}
       | {ADJACENT DUPLICATES FROM itab
          [COMPARING comp1 comp2 ...|{ALL FIELDS}]} }.
```

Effect

Deletes lines from an internal table `itab`.

Additions

- `TABLE itab FROM wa`
  Specifies a line to be deleted by corresponding to the key values of a work area `wa`.

- `TABLE itab WITH TABLE KEY comp_name1|(name1) = dobj1 comp_name2|(name2) = dobj2 ...`
  Specifies a line to be deleted by statically or dynamically indicating the components of a table key.
- `itab INDEX idx`
  Specifies a line to be deleted by indicating the table index `idx`.
- `itab [FROM idx1] [TO idx2] [WHERE log_exp]`
  Specifies multiple lines to be deleted by indicating a lower and upper table index `idx1` and `idx2` and by limiting these indexes with a condition *log_exp* (see `log_exp` entry).
- `ADJACENT DUPLICATES FROM itab [COMPARING comp1 comp2 ...|{ALL FIELDS}]`
  Specifies identical adjacent lines where the relevant comparison components are specified with `COMPARING`.

DELETE FROM

Syntax

```
DELETE FROM { {MEMORY ID id}
            | {DATABASE      dbtab(ar) [CLIENT cl] ID id}
            | {SHARED MEMORY dbtab(ar) [CLIENT cl] ID id}
            | {SHARED BUFFER dbtab(ar) [CLIENT cl] ID id} }.
```

Effect

Deletes the data cluster of the ID specified in `id`.

Additions

- `MEMORY`
  Specifies a data cluster in the ABAP memory.
- `DATABASE dbtab(ar) [CLIENT cl]`
  Specifies a data cluster in a database table `dbtab` in the `ar` area and a client ID `cl`.
- `SHARED BUFFER dbtab(ar) [CLIENT cl]`
  Specifies a data cluster in an application buffer with an automatic displacement mechanism in the shared memory of the application server. This shared memory is addressed via the name of a database table `dbtab`, an area `ar` and a client ID `cl`.

Addition since Release 6.10

- `SHARED MEMORY dbtab(ar) [CLIENT cl]`
  Specifies a data cluster in an application buffer with manual displacement mechanism in the application server's shared memory, which is addressed via the name of a database table `dbtab`, an area `ar` and a client ID `cl`.

D

DEMAND

Syntax

```
DEMAND val1 = f1 val2 = f2 ...
       FROM CONTEXT context_ref
       [MESSAGES INTO itab].
```

Release

Obsolete

Effect

Assigns the derived values `val1 val2 ...` of a context instance that is referenced by `context_ref` to the data objects `f1 f2 ...`

Addition

- `MESSAGES INTO itab`
  Appends context messages to the internal table `itab`. Without this addition messages are sent.

DESCRIBE DISTANCE

Syntax

```
DESCRIBE DISTANCE BETWEEN dobj1 AND dobj2 INTO dst
                          IN {BYTE|CHARACTER} MODE.
```

Effect

Determines the distance in bytes or characters between two data objects `dobj1` and `dobj2` in the memory and returns the result in `dst`.

Addition since Release 6.10

- `IN {BYTE|CHARACTER} MODE`
  Defines whether the distance is determined in bytes or characters.

DESCRIBE FIELD

Syntax

```
DESCRIBE FIELD dobj
  [TYPE typ [COMPONENTS com]]
  [LENGTH ilen IN {BYTE|CHARACTER} MODE]
  [DECIMALS dec]
  [OUTPUT-LENGTH olen]
  [HELP-ID hlp]
  [EDIT MASK mask].
```

Effect

Determines the properties of a data object `dobj`.

Additions

- `TYPE typ [COMPONENTS com]`
  Returns the data type in `typ` and the number of components in `com`.
- `LENGTH ilen`
  Returns the length in `ilen`.
- `DECIMALS dec`
  Returns the number of fractional portions in `dec`.
- `OUTPUT-LENGTH olen`
  Returns the screen output length in `olen`.
- `HELP-ID hlp`
  Returns the name of the data element in the ABAP dictionary that is referenced by the type of `dobj`, in `hlp`.
- `EDIT MASK mask`
  Returns the name of the conversion routine in the ABAP dictionary that is assigned to the type of `dobj`, in `mask`.

Addition since Release 6.10

- `IN {BYTE|CHARACTER} MODE`
  Defines whether the length is determined in bytes or characters.

DESCRIBE LIST

Syntax

```
DESCRIBE LIST { {NUMBER OF {LINES|PAGES} n}
              | {LINE linno PAGE page}
              | {PAGE pagno [LINE-SIZE width]
```

```
                             [LINE-COUNT length]
                             [LINES lines]
                             [FIRST-LINE first_line]
                             [TOP-LINES top_lines]
                             [TITLE-LINES title_lines]
                             [HEAD-LINES header_lines]
                             [END-LINES footer_lines]} }
               [INDEX idx].
```

D

Effect

Determines the properties of a list in the list buffer.

Additions

- `NUMBER OF {LINES|PAGES} n`
  Returns the number of lines or pages in `n`.
- `LINE linno PAGE page`
  Returns the page of the row specified in `linno` in `page`.
- `PAGE pagno`
  Returns properties of the page specified in `pagno`:
  - `LINE-SIZE width`—Line width
  - `LINE-COUNT length`—Page length
  - `LINES lines`—Number of lines
  - `FIRST-LINE first_line`—Line number of the first line
  - `TOP-LINES top_lines`—Number of header lines
  - `TITLE-LINES title_lines`—Number of title lines
  - `HEAD-LINES header_lines`—Number of column header lines
  - `END-LINES footer_lines`—Number of footer lines
- `INDEX idx`
  Specifies the list index in `idx`. If no index is specified, either the basic list or the list in which a list event took place is evaluated.

DESCRIBE TABLE

Syntax

```
DESCRIBE TABLE itab [KIND knd] [LINES lin] [OCCURS n].
```

Effect

Determines the properties of an internal table `itab`.

Additions

- `KIND knd`
  Returns the table type in `knd`.
- `LINES lin`
  Returns the number of lines in `lin`.
- `OCCURS n`
  Returns the initial memory allocation in `n`.

DETAIL

Syntax

```
DETAIL.
```

Release

Obsolete

Effect

Specifies the intensity of the background color of a list.

DIVIDE

Syntax

```
DIVIDE dobj1 BY dobj2.
```

Effect

Divides the content of `dobj1` by the content of `dobj2` and assigns the result to `dobj1`.

DIVIDE-CORRESPONDING

Syntax

```
DIVIDE-CORRESPONDING struc1 BY struc2.
```

Release

Obsolete

Effect

Divides the components of a structure `struc1` by components having the same name of a structure `struc2`.

DO

Syntax

```
DO [n TIMES]
   [VARYING dobj FROM dobj1 NEXT dobj2 [RANGE range]].
  [statement_block]
ENDDO.
```

Effect

Executes the statement `statement_block` several times within a loop.

Addition

- `n TIMES`
  Limits the number of loop passes to `n`.

Addition since Release 6.10

- `RANGE range`
  The data object `range` restricts the memory area that can be addressed with `VARYING`.

Obsolete addition

- `VARYING dobj FROM dobj1 NEXT dobj2`
  Assigns a value of the memory sequence defined by `dobj1` and `dobj2` to a variable `dobj` during each loop pass.

EDITOR-CALL

Syntax

```
EDITOR-CALL FOR { {REPORT prog [DISPLAY-MODE]}
                | {itab [TITLE title]
                        [{DISPLAY-MODE}
                        |{BACKUP INTO jtab}]} }.
```

Effect

Calls the ABAP Editor for a program `prog`.

Addition

- `DISPLAY-MODE`
  Opens the ABAP Editor in display mode.

Obsolete Additions

- `FOR itab`
  Calls the ABAP Editor as text editor for any text in an internal table `itab`.

- `TITLE title`
  Displays the title `title` in the title bar of the text editor.
- `BACKUP INTO jtab`
  Assigns the content of `itab` to the table `jtab` before the editor is launched.

END-OF-PAGE

Syntax

```
END-OF-PAGE.
```

Effect

Initiates an event block whose event is triggered during the creation of a basic list when the page footer is reached.

END-OF-SELECTION

Syntax

```
END-OF-SELECTION.
```

Effect

Initiates an event block whose event is triggered in executable programs once the related logical database has read out all data.

ENHANCEMENT

Syntax

```
ENHANCEMENT id.
  ...
ENDENHANCEMENT.
```

Release

7.0

Effect

Implements a source code enhancement as a source code plug-in of the ID `id`.

ENHANCEMENT-POINT

Syntax

```
ENHANCEMENT-POINT enh_id SPOTS spot1 spot2 ...
                  [STATIC]
                  [INCLUDE BOUND].
```

Release

7.0

Effect

Defines a specific point in the source code as enhancement option of the ID `enh_id` for a source code enhancement via source code plug-ins and assigns it to single enhancement spots `spot1`, `spot2`, ...

Additions

- `STATIC`
  Defines a static enhancement option.
- `INCLUDE BOUND`
  Bincs the enhancement option to the current include program.

ENHANCEMENT-SECTION

Syntax

```
ENHANCEMENT-SECTION enh_id SPOTS spot1 spot2 ...
                    [STATIC]
                    [INCLUDE BOUND].
  ...
END-ENHANCEMENT-SECTION.
```

Release

7.0

Effect

Defines a section in the source code as enhancement option of the ID `enh_id` for a source code enhancement via a source code plug-in and assigns it to single enhancement spots `spot1`, `spot2`, ...

Additions

- `STATIC`
  Defines a static enhancement option.
- `INCLUDE BOUND`
  Binds the enhancement option to the current include program.

EVENTS

Syntax

```
EVENTS evt [ EXPORTING VALUE(p1) typing
                          [OPTIONAL|{DEFAULT def1}]
                        VALUE(p2) typing
                          [OPTIONAL|{DEFAULT def2}]
                         ... ].
```

Effect

Declares an instance event `evt` of a class or an interface.

Additions

- `EXPORTING VALUE(p1) ... VALUE(p2) ...`
  Defines the output parameters `p1 p2 ...` of the event.
- *`typing`*
  Types the output parameters. See `typing` entry.
- `OPTIONAL|DEFAULT`
  Determines optional output parameters either without or with default parameters `def1 def2 ...`

EXEC SQL

Syntax

```
EXEC SQL [PERFORMING subr].
  ...
ENDEXEC.
```

Effect

Defines an area in which native SQL statements for database accesses can be listed.

Obsolete addition

- `PERFORMING subr`
  Implicit cursor processing if a `SELECT` statement is specified; for each row that is read the subroutine `subr` is called.

EXIT

Syntax

```
EXIT.
```

Release

Obsolete outside loops since 6.10.

Effect

Leaves a loop or processing block. Within a loop, the entire loop processing is left, and the subsequent loop is executed. Outside a loop, the current processing block is left.

EXIT FROM SQL

Syntax

```
EXIT FROM SQL.
```

Release

Obsolete

Effect

Cancels the implicit cursor processing on `EXEC SQL`. The processing continues after `ENDEXEC`.

EXIT FROM STEP-LOOP

Syntax

```
EXIT FROM STEP-LOOP.
```

Effect

Leaves the loop processing of a table control or step loop in the current dynpro. The processing continues with the dynpro flow logic after the loop.

EXPORT

Syntax

```
EXPORT { {p1 = dobj1 p2 = dobj2 ...}
       | {p1 FROM dobj1 p2 FROM dobj2 ...}
       | (ptab) }
  TO { {DATA BUFFER xstr}
     | {INTERNAL TABLE itab}
     | {MEMORY ID id}
     | {DATABASE      dbtab(ar) [FROM wa] [CLIENT cl] ID id}
     | {SHARED MEMORY dbtab(ar) [FROM wa] [CLIENT cl] ID id}
```

```
| {SHARED BUFFER dbtab(ar) [FROM wa] [CLIENT cl] ID id} }
[ COMPRESSION { ON | OFF } ].
```

Effect

Stores data objects `dobj1 dobj2 ...` in a data cluster.

Additions

- `{p1 = dobj1 p2 = dobj2 ...}|{p1 FROM dobj1 p2 FROM dobj2 ...}|(ptab)`
  Defines the data cluster either statically by listing single parameters via `p1 = dobj1 p2 = dobj2 ...` or `p1 FROM dobj1 p2 FROM dobj2 ...` or dynamically by specifying them in an internal table `ptab`.
- `MEMORY`
  Stores the data cluster in the ABAP memory.
- `DATABASE dbtab(ar) [CLIENT cl]`
  Stores the data cluster in a database table `dbtab` in the `ar` area and a client ID `cl`.
- `SHARED BUFFER dbtab(ar) [CLIENT cl]`
  Stores the data cluster in an application buffer with automatic displacement mechanism in the shared memory of the application server. The shared memory is addressed via the name of a database table `dbtab`, an area `ar` and a client ID `cl`.
- `ID id`
  Specifies the data cluster ID in `id`.
- `FROM wa`
  Specifies a work area `wa` with additional information on the data cluster.
- `COMPRESSION { ON | OFF }`
  Specifies whether the data cluster is stored in compressed format or not.

Additions ab Release 6.10

- `DATA BUFFER xstr`
  Stores the data cluster as byte string in `xstr`.
- `SHARED MEMORY dbtab(ar) [CLIENT cl]`
  Stores the data cluster in an application buffer with manual displacement mechanism in the shared memory of the application server. The shared memory is addressed via the name of a database table `dbtab`, an area `ar`, and a client ID `cl`.

Addition since Release 6.20

- `INTERNAL TABLE itab`
  Stores the data cluster in an internal table `itab`.

EXTRACT

Syntax

```
EXTRACT [ header | field_group ].
```

Effect

Appends a field group declared with `FIELD-GROUPS` to the extract dataset of the program.

FETCH

Syntax

```
FETCH NEXT CURSOR dbcur
  { { INTO { {[CORRESPONDING FIELDS OF] wa}
           | (dobj1, dobj2, ...) } }
  | { INTO|APPENDING [CORRESPONDING FIELDS OF] TABLE itab
                     [PACKAGE SIZE n] } } .
```

Effect

Fetches rows from the resulting set of a database cursor opened with `OPEN CURSOR`.

Additions

- `INTO wa`
  Reads a row and assigns it to a work area `wa`.
- `INTO (dobj1, dobj2, ...)`
  Reads a row and assigns it to multiple data objects `dobj1, dobj2, ...`
- `INTO|APPENDING TABLE itab`
  Reads multiple rows and assigns them to an internal table `itab` or appends them to it.
- `CORRESPONDING FIELDS OF`
  Restricts the transport to components of the work area `wa` or the internal table `itab` having the same name.
- `PACKAGE SIZE n`
  Passes the rows in packages of `n` rows on to the internal table `itab`.

FIELD-GROUPS

Syntax

```
FIELD-GROUPS [ header | field_group ].
```

Effect

Declares a field group for the extract dataset of the program, which either gets the predefined name `header` or any other name `field_group`. The structure of the field group can be defined with `INSERT`.

FIELD-SYMBOLS

Syntax

```
FIELD-SYMBOLS <fs> { typing
                   | {STRUCTURE struc DEFAULT dobj} }.
```

Effect

Declares a field symbol `<fs>`. The angle brackets are part of the designator.

Addition

- *`typing`*
  Types the field symbol. See `typing` entry.

Obsolete addition

- `STRUCTURE struc DEFAULT dobj`
  Imposes a structure `struc` and assigns a data object `dobj`.

FIELDS

Syntax

```
FIELDS dobj.
```

Release

Obsolete

Effect

Addresses a data object `dobj` to avoid a warning of the extended program check, if the data object is not addressed statically.

FIND

Syntax

```
FIND [{FIRST OCCURRENCE}|{ALL OCCURRENCES} OF]
     {[SUBSTRING] sub_string} | {REGEX regex} IN
     { {[SECTION [OFFSET off] [LENGTH len] OF] dobj}
     | {TABLE itab [FROM lin1 [OFFSET off1]]
                   [TO   lin2 [OFFSET off2]]} }
     [IN {BYTE|CHARACTER} MODE]
     [{RESPECTING|IGNORING} CASE]
     [MATCH COUNT  mcnt]
     { {[MATCH LINE   mlin]
        [MATCH OFFSET moff]
        [MATCH LENGTH mlen]}
     | [RESULTS result_tab|result_wa] }
     [SUBMATCHES s1 s2 ...].
```

F

Release

6.10

Effect

Searches for byte strings or character strings or for regular expressions in a byte or character-like data object dobj or in an internal table itab.

Additions

- sub_string
  Specifies a substring to be searched for.
- SECTION [OFFSET off] [LENGTH len] OF dobj
  Searches within a byte string or character string dobj where the search area is limited to the section starting from the offset specified in off and with the length specified in len.
- IN {BYTE|CHARACTER} MODE
  Determines byte or character string processing.
- {RESPECTING|IGNORING} CASE
  Determines whether uppercase and lowercase letters are considered in sub_string, regex and dobj.
- MATCH OFFSET moff
  Returns the offset of the last found match in moff.
- MATCH LENGTH mlen
  Returns the length of the last found substring in mlen.

Additions since Release 7.0

- `{[SUBSTRING] sub_string} | {REGEX regex}`
  Determines whether a substring `substring` or a regular expression `regex` is searched for (see pages 187–189).
- `{FIRST OCCURRENCE}|{ALL OCCURRENCES OF}`
  Determines whether the first occurrence or all occurrences are searched for.
- `TABLE itab [FROM lin1 [OFFSET off1]] [TO lin2 [OFFSET off2]]`
  Searches in an internal table `itab` where the search area is restricted to the section beginning with the line specified in `lin1` and the offset specified in `off1`, up to and including the line specified in `lin2` and the offset specified in `off2`.
- `MATCH COUNT mcnt`
  Returns the number of found matches in `mcnt`.
- `MATCH LINE mlin`
  Returns the line number of the last found match in `mlin` when searching within internal tables.
- `RESULTS result_tab|result_wa`
  Returns the properties of all found matches or of the last found match in an internal table `result_tab` or in a structure `result_wa` of the MATCH_RESULT type.
- `SUBMATCHES s1 s2 ...`
  Returns the contents of the subgroup registers of the last found match in `s1`, `s2`, ... during a search for regular expressions.

FORM

Syntax

```
FORM subr
  [ TABLES
      { t1 [{TYPE itab_type}|{LIKE itab}|{STRUCTURE struc}]
        t2 [{TYPE itab_type}|{LIKE itab}|{STRUCTURE struc}]
        ... } ]
  [ USING
      { {VALUE(u1)}|u1 [typing|{STRUCTURE struc}]
        {VALUE(u2)}|u2 [typing|{STRUCTURE struc}]
        ... } ]
  [ CHANGING
      { {VALUE(c1)}|c1 [typing|{STRUCTURE struc}]
```

```
        {VALUE(c2)}|c2 [typing|{STRUCTURE struc}]
        ... } ]
    [ RAISING exc1 exc2 ... ].
    ...
ENDFORM.
```

F

Effect

Defines a subroutine `subr`. The subroutine is defined with `FORM` and implemented between `FORM` and `ENDFORM`.

Additions

- `USING`
  Defines input parameters `u1 u2 ...`
- `CHANGING`
  Defines input/output parameters `c1 c2 ...`
- `VALUE`
  Defines pass by value for a formal parameter. Without the `VALUE` addition the pass by reference is defined.
- *`typing`*
  Types the formal parameters. See `typing` entry.

Addition since Release 6.10

- `RAISING exc1 exc2 ...`
  Declares class-based exceptions `exc1 exc2 ...` that can be propagated from the subroutine.

Obsolete Additions

- `TABLES`
  Defines table parameters `t1 t2 ...`
- `STRUCTURE struc`
  Imposes a structure `struc` onto a formal parameter.

FORMAT

Syntax

```
FORMAT [COLOR { { { { COL_BACKGROUND
                    | {1 | COL_HEADING }
                    | {2 | COL_NORMAL }
                    | {3 | COL_TOTAL }
                    | {4 | COL_KEY }
                    | {5 | COL_POSITIVE }
```

```
                 | {6 | COL_NEGATIVE }
                 | {7 | COL_GROUP } } [ON] }
               | OFF}
           | {= col} }]
    [INTENSIFIED [ {ON|OFF} | {= flag} ]]
    [INVERSE     [ {ON|OFF} | {= flag} ]]
    [HOTSPOT     [ {ON|OFF} | {= flag} ]]
    [INPUT       [ {ON|OFF} | {= flag} ]]
    [FRAMES      [ {ON|OFF} | {= flag} ]]
    [RESET].
```

Effect

Formats a section of a list.

Additions

- `ON | OFF | {= flag}`
  Switches a format on and off. In `flag` the value is checked for 0 or other than 0.
- `COLOR`
  Sets the color:
  - `COL_BACKGROUND`—GUI-dependent
  - `1 | COL_HEADING`—Gray-blue
  - `2 | COL_NORMAL`—Light gray
  - `3 | COL_TOTAL`—Yellow
  - `4 | COL_KEY`—Blue-green
  - `5 | COL_POSITIVE`—Green
  - `6 | COL_NEGATIVE`—Red
  - `7 | COL_GROUP`—Violet
  - `= col`—dynamic indication of a color ID in `col`.
- `INTENSIFIED`
  Sets the intensity of the background color.
- `INVERSE`
  Toggles between foreground and background colors.
- `HOTSPOT`
  Creates a hotspot to respond to single mouse clicks.
- `INPUT`
  Creates an input area.

- `RESET`
  Sets all settings except `FRAMES` to the `OFF` status.

Addition since Release 6.10

- `FRAMES`
  Controls the conversion of "-" and "|" into line elements.

F

FREE

Syntax

```
FREE dobj.
```

Effect

Initializes a data object `dobj` by assigning the type-specific initial value. For internal tables, the entire memory area allocated by lines will be released.

FREE MEMORY

Syntax

```
FREE MEMORY ID id.
```

Effect

Deletes the data cluster of the ID specified in `id` from the ABAP memory.

FREE OBJECT—OLE

Syntax

```
FREE OBJECT ole [NO FLUSH].
```

Effect

Releases the memory of an automation object `ole` created with `CREATE OBJECT ole` on the presentation server.

Addition

- `NO FLUSH`
  Defines that the release request isn't passed on to the presentation layer until the function module FLUSH is called or the screen is changed.

FUNCTION

Syntax

```
FUNCTION func.
  ...
ENDFUNCTION.
```

Effect

Implements a function module func. A function module is defined in the function builder and implemented between FUNCTION and ENDFUNCTION.

FUNCTION-POOL

Syntax

```
FUNCTION-POOL fpool [NO STANDARD PAGE HEADING]
                    [LINE-SIZE width]
                    [LINE-COUNT page_lines[(footer_lines)]]
                    [MESSAGE-ID mid].
```

Effect

Initiates a function pool fpool.

Additions

- NO STANDARD PAGE HEADING
  Suppresses the output of the standard page header.
- LINE-SIZE width
  Sets the line width of the program's lists to width characters.
- LINE-COUNT page_lines[(footer_lines)]
  Sets the page length of the program's basic list to page_lines lines and reserves footer_lines footer lines.
- MESSAGE-ID mid
  Determines a message class mid for short forms of MESSAGE.

GENERATE SUBROUTINE POOL

Syntax

```
GENERATE SUBROUTINE POOL itab NAME prog
  [MESSAGE mess]
  [INCLUDE incl]
```

```
  [LINE line]
  [WORD wrd]
  [OFFSET off]
  [MESSAGE-ID mid]
  [SHORTDUMP-ID sid].
```

G

Effect

Generates a temporary subroutine pool from the content of an internal table itab. The name of subroutine pool is returned in prog.

Additions

- MESSAGE mess
  Returns the first error message in mess in the case of a syntax error.
- INCLUDE incl
  Returns the name of the include program in which a syntax error occurs in incl.
- LINE line
  Returns the first line that contains a syntax error in line.
- WORD wrd
  Returns the first word that contains a syntax error in wrd.
- OFFSET off
  Returns the offset of the first syntax error in a line in off.
- MESSAGE-ID mid
  Returns the key of the first syntax error message from the TRMSG table in mid.
- SHORTDUMP-ID sid
  Returns the generation error ID from the SNAPT table in sid.

GET

Syntax

```
GET node [LATE] [FIELDS f1 f2 ...].
```

Effect

Initiates an event block whose event is triggered during the readout of datasets of the node node by a logical database.

Additions

- `LATE`
  Event when the logical database has read all datasets of the node `node`.
- `FIELDS f1 f2 ...`
  Specifies which fields are read by the logical database.

GET BADI

Syntax

```
GET BADI badi [FILTERS f1 = x1 f2 = x2 ...]
              [CONTEXT con].
```

Release

7.0

Effect

Places a BAdI reference to a BAdI object into a BAdI reference variable.

Additions

- `FILTERS f1 = x1 f2 = x2 ...`
  Specifies a setting `x1`, `x2`, ... for the filters `f1`, `f2`, ... of the BAdI to search for BAdI implementations.
- `CONTEXT con`
  Specifies a BAdI context object.

GET BIT

Syntax

```
GET BIT bitpos OF byte_string INTO val.
```

Effect

Returns the bit in the bit position `bitpos` of the data object `byte_string` in `val`.

GET CURSOR

Syntax

```
GET CURSOR { { FIELD field
                [VALUE val]
                [LENGTH len]
                [[DISPLAY|MEMORY] OFFSET off]
                [LINE line]
                [AREA area] }
           | { LINE line
                [VALUE val]
                [LENGTH len]
                [[DISPLAY|MEMORY] OFFSET off] } }.
```

G

Effect

Evaluates the cursor position in screens and lists.

Additions

- `FIELD field`
  Returns the name of the screen element or of the field included in a list in `field`, and identifies additional field-specific properties of the cursor position:
  - `VALUE val`—Returns the value of the screen element or of the output area of a list in `val`.
  - `LENGTH len`—Returns the length of the screen element or of the output area of a list in `len`.
  - `OFFSET off`—Returns the offset of the cursor in the screen element or in the output area of a list in `off`.
  - `LINE line`—Returns the line number of a table control, a step loop or the list in `line`.
  - `AREA area`—Returns the name of a table control in `area`.
- `LINE line`
  Returns the line number of a table control, a step loop or of the list in `line`, and identifies additional line-specific properties of the cursor position in lists:
  - `VALUE val`—Returns the value of the list line in `val`.
  - `LENGTH len`—Returns the length of the list line in `len`.
  - `OFFSET off`—Returns the offset of the cursor in the list line in `off`.

Addition since Release 6.20

- `DISPLAY|MEMORY`
  Differentiates between screen position and list buffer position in lists.

GET DATASET

Syntax

```
GET DATASET dset [POSITION pos] [ATTRIBUTES attr].
```

Release

6.10

Effect

Returns the properties of a file opened with `OPEN DATASET`.

Additions

- `POSITION pos`
  Returns the current position of the file pointer in `pos`.
- `ATTRIBUTES attr`
  Returns the properties of the file in the `attr` structure of the DSET_ATTRIBUTES type.

GET LOCALE

Syntax

```
GET LOCALE LANGUAGE lang COUNTRY cntry MODIFIER mod.
```

Effect

Returns the current text environment.

Additions

- `LANGUAGE lang`
  Returns the language key in `lang`.
- `COUNTRY cntry`
  Returns the country key in `cntry`.
- `MODIFIER mod`
  Returns the ID of a specific locale in `mod`.

GET PARAMETER

Syntax

```
GET PARAMETER ID pid FIELD dobj.
```

Effect

Returns the value of the SPA/GPA parameter specified in pid in the SAP memory in dobj.

G

GET PF-STATUS

Syntax

```
GET PF-STATUS status [PROGRAM prog] [EXCLUDING fcode].
```

Effect

Returns the current GUI status in status.

Additions

- PROGRAM prog
  Returns the program in which the GUI status is defined, in prog.
- EXCLUDING fcode
  Returns the inactive function codes in the internal table fcode.

GET PROPERTY

Syntax

```
GET PROPERTY OF ole attr = dobj [NO FLUSH] [QUEUE-ONLY].
```

Effect

Assigns the content of the attribute attr of an automation object ole created with CREATE OBJECT ole to the data object dobj.

Additions

- NO FLUSH
  Defines that the attribute isn't adopted by the presentation layer until the function module FLUSH is called or the screen is changed.
- QUEUE-ONLY
  Defines that during a flush the return values of the automation queue methods called with CALL METHOD OF are not written to the data objects rc.

GET REFERENCE

Syntax

```
GET REFERENCE OF dobj INTO dref.
```

Effect

Returns a reference to the data object dobj in the reference variable dref.

GET RUN TIME

Syntax

```
GET RUN TIME FIELD rtime.
```

Effect

Returns the program runtime since the first execution of the statement in rtime, measured in microseconds.

GET TIME

Syntax

```
GET TIME [FIELD tim].
```

Effect

Updates the system fields sy-datlo, sy-datum, sy-timlo, sy-uzeit and sy-zonlo.

Additions

- FIELD tim
  Returns the current time in tim without updating the system fields.

GET TIME STAMP

Syntax

```
GET TIME STAMP FIELD time_stamp.
```

Effect

Returns the current time stamp in time_stamp of type TIMESTAMP or TIMESTAMPL.

HIDE

Syntax

```
HIDE dobj.
```

Effect

Saves the content of the dobj variable with the current list line in the current list level.

H
I

IF

Syntax

```
IF log_exp1.
  [statement_block1]
[ELSEIF log_exp2.
  [statement_block2]]
...
[ELSE.
  [statement_blockn]]
ENDIF.
```

Effect

Defines a control structure with multiple statement blocks statement_block1 ... statement_blockn. The statement block after the first true logical expression *log_exp1 log_exp2* ... (see log_exp entry) is executed. If none of the logical expressions is true, the statement block after the ELSE statement is executed.

IMPORT

Syntax

```
IMPORT { {p1 = dobj1 p2 = dobj2 ...}
       | {p1 TO dobj1  p2 TO dobj2 ...}
       | (ptab) }
  FROM
   { {DATA BUFFER xstr}
   | {INTERNAL TABLE itab}
   | {MEMORY ID id}
   | {DATABASE      dbtab(ar) [TO wa] [CLIENT cl]
                                        {(ID id}
```

```
                                  |{MAJOR-ID id1
                                   [MINOR-ID id2]}}}
 | {SHARED MEMORY dbtab(ar) [TO wa] [CLIENT cl] ID id}
 | {SHARED BUFFER dbtab(ar) [TO wa] [CLIENT cl] ID id} }
 [ { { { {[ACCEPTING PADDING] [ACCEPTING TRUNCATION]}
       |  [IGNORING STRUCTURE BOUNDARIES] }
       [ IGNORING CONVERSION ERRORS
         [REPLACEMENT CHARACTER rc] ] }
   | [IN CHAR-TO-HEX MODE] } ]
 [CODEPAGE INTO cp]
 [ENDIAN INTO endian].
```

Effect

Imports a data cluster into data objects `dobj1 dobj2 ...`

Additions

- `{p1 = dobj1 p2 = dobj2 ...}|{p1 TO dobj1 p2 TO dobj2 ...}|(ptab)`
  Selects the data to be read out either statically by listing individual parameters via `p1 = dobj1 p2 = dobj2 ...` or `p1 TO dobj1 p2 TO dobj2 ...`, or dynamically by specifying them in an internal table `ptab`.
- `MEMORY`
  Specifies a data cluster stored in the ABAP memory.
- `DATABASE dbtab(ar) [CLIENT cl]`
  Specifies a data cluster stored in a database table `dbtab` in the `ar` area and a client ID `cl`.
- `SHARED BUFFER dbtab(ar) [CLIENT cl]`
  Specifies a data cluster stored in an application buffer with automatic displacement mechanism in the shared memory of the application server. The shared memory is addressed via the name of a database table `dbtab`, an area `ar` and a client ID `cl`.
- `ID id`
  Specifies the data cluster ID in `id`.
- `TO wa`
  Specifies a work area `wa` to receive information on the data cluster.

Additions since Release 6.10

- `DATA BUFFER xstr`
  Specifies a data cluster stored as a byte string in `xstr`.

- `SHARED MEMORY dbtab(ar) [CLIENT cl]`
  Specifies a data cluster stored in an application buffer with manual displacement mechanism in the application server's shared memory, which is addressed via the name of a database table `dbtab`, an area `ar` and a client ID `cl`.
- `ACCEPTING PADDING`
  Permits the readout into longer target fields.
- `ACCEPTING TRUNCATION`
  Permits the readout into shorter target fields.
- `IGNORING STRUCTURE BOUNDARIES`
  Permits the readout into differently structured structures.
- `IGNORING CONVERSION ERRORS [REPLACEMENT CHARACTER rc]`
  Suppresses an untreatable exception during the conversion into the target code page, where `rc` represents a replacement character for non-convertible characters.
- `IN CHAR-TO-HEX MODE`
  Permits the readout of character-type data into byte strings.
- `CODEPAGE INTO cp`
  Returns the code page of the data cluster in `cp`.
- `ENDIAN INTO endian`
  Returns the endian of the data cluster in `endian`.

Addition since Release 6.20

- `INTERNAL TABLE itab`
  Specifies a data cluster stored in an internal table `itab`.

Addition since Release 6.40

- `ACCEPTING PADDING|TRUNCATION, IGNORING STRUCTURE BOUNDARIES`
  In combination with `SHARED BUFFER`.

Obsolete addition

- `MAJOR-ID id1 [MINOR-ID id2]`
  Specifies the ID `id` of a data cluster in database tables by means of a template.

IMPORT DIRECTORY

Syntax

```
IMPORT DIRECTORY INTO itab
  FROM DATABASE dbtab(ar) [TO wa] [CLIENT cl] ID id.
```

Effect

Reads the table of contents of a data cluster into an internal table itab.

Additions

- FROM DATABASE dbtab(ar) [CLIENT cl]
  Specifies a data cluster stored in a database table dbtab in the ar area including the client ID cl.
- ID id
  Specifies the ID id of the data cluster.
- TO wa
  Specifies a work area wa to receive information on the data cluster.

INCLUDE

Syntax

```
INCLUDE incl [IF FOUND].
```

Effect

Includes the include program incl at the current source code position.

Addition since Release 6.40

- IF FOUND
  Suppresses the syntax check error message, if the include program is not found.

INCLUDE—TYPE, STRUCTURE

Syntax

```
INCLUDE { {TYPE struc_type} | {STRUCTURE struc} }
        [AS name [RENAMING WITH SUFFIX suffix]].
```

Effect

Includes in a structure definition all components of the structured type struc_type or of the structure struc at the current position.

Additions

- AS name
  Defines a superordinate name name for the included components.

- `RENAMING WITH SUFFIX suffix`
  Renames the included components by attaching the suffix `suffix`.

INFOTYPES

Syntax

```
INFOTYPES nnnn [NAME name]
               [OCCURS n]
               [MODE N]
               [VALID FROM intlim1 TO intlim2]
               [AS PERSON TABLE].
```

Release

Obsolete

Effect

Creates an internal table called `pnnnn` for an infotype of the SAP ERP HR component.

Additions

- `nnnn`
  Four-digit numeric key of an infotype.
- `NAME name`
  Defines the name of the internal table as `name`.
- `OCCURS n`
  Defines the initial memory allocation for the internal table.
- `MODE N`
  Prevents linking to special logical databases.
- `VALID FROM intlim1 TO intlim2`
  Defines the columns `intlim1` and `intlim2` as interval limits for the obsolete short form of `PROVIDE`.

Addition since Release 6.20

- `AS PERSON TABLE`
  Defines the name of the internal table as `ppnnnn`.

INITIALIZATION

Syntax

```
INITIALIZATION.
```

Effect
Initiates an event block whose event is triggered in an executable program between LOAD-OF-PROGRAM and the selection screen processing.

INPUT

Syntax

```
INPUT.
```

Release
Obsolete

Effect
Creates an input area in a list.

INSERT dbtab

Syntax

```
INSERT { {INTO {dbtab|(dbtab_syntax)} [CLIENT SPECIFIED]
          VALUES wa}
        | {{dbtab|(dbtab_syntax)} [CLIENT SPECIFIED]
          FROM wa|{TABLE itab [ACCEPTING DUPLICATE KEYS]}} }.
```

Effect
Inserts rows in a database table.

Additions

- INTO {dbtab|(dbtab_syntax)}
  Specifies the database table statically or dynamically.
- CLIENT SPECIFIED
  Switches off the automatic client handling.
- {VALUES wa}|{FROM wa}|{FROM TABLE itab}
  Specifies the rows to be inserted as work area wa or as lines of an internal table itab.
- ACCEPTING DUPLICATE KEYS
  Suppresses an exception, if existing rows are to be inserted.

Addition since Release 6.10

- (dbtab_syntax)
  In addition to flat character-type fields, strings and internal tables with a character-type line type can also be specified.

INSERT field-group

Syntax

```
INSERT dobj1 dobj2 ... INTO { header | field_group }.
```

Effect

Builds up the structure of a field group that was defined with FIELD-GROUPS for the extract dataset of the program, from global data objects dobj1 dobj2 ...

INSERT itab

Syntax

```
INSERT { wa
       | {INITIAL LINE}
       | {LINES OF jtab [FROM idx1] [TO idx2]} }
  INTO { {TABLE itab}
       | {itab INDEX idx} }
       [ {ASSIGNING <fs> [CASTING]}|{REFERENCE INTO dref} ].
```

Effect

Inserts lines into an internal table itab.

Additions

- wa
  Inserts a work area wa.
- INITIAL LINE
  Inserts an initial line.
- LINES OF jtab [FROM idx1] [TO idx2]
  Inserts lines determined by the indices idx1 and idx2 from the internal table jtab.
- INTO TABLE itab
  Determines the insertion point via the table key.
- INTO itab INDEX idx
  Determines the insertion point via the table index idx.

Additions since Release 6.10

- ASSIGNING <fs>
  Assigns an inserted single line to a field symbol <fs>.

- REFERENCE INTO dref
  Assigns a reference to an inserted single line to the reference variable dref.

Addition since Release 7.0

- CASTING
  Casts the line to the typing of the field symbol.

INSERT REPORT

Syntax

```
INSERT REPORT prog FROM itab
              [MAXIMUM WIDTH INTO wid]
              { [KEEPING DIRECTORY ENTRY]
              | { [PROGRAM TYPE pt]
                  [FIXED-POINT ARITHMETIC fp]
                  [UNICODE ENABLING uc] }
              | [DIRECTORY ENTRY dir] }.
```

Effect

Inserts the source code contained in the internal table itab as an ABAP program prog into the repository.

Additions since Release 6.10

- MAXIMUM WIDTH INTO wid
  Returns the number of characters of the longest source code line that was passed on, in wid.
- KEEPING DIRECTORY ENTRY
  Keeps the properties of an existing program.
- PROGRAM TYPE pt
  Determines the program type by the specification in pt.
- FIXED-POINT ARITHMETIC fp
  Determines the fixed point arithmetic by the specification in fp.
- UNICODE ENABLING uc
  Determines the Unicode check by the specification in uc.
- DIRECTORY ENTRY dir
  Determines the program properties according to the specifications in the structure dir of the TRDIR type.

INSERT TEXTPOOL

Syntax

```
INSERT TEXTPOOL prog FROM itab LANGUAGE lang.
```

Effect

Inserts the text elements contained in the internal table itab of the TEXTPOOL type as a text pool of the language specified in lang for the program specified in prog into the repository.

I

INTERFACE

Syntax

```
INTERFACE intf.
  [components]
ENDINTERFACE.
```

Effect

Declares an interface intf. Within the declaration, the components components of the interface are declared with ALIASES, [CLASS-]DATA, [CLASS-]METHODS and [CLASS-]EVENTS.

INTERFACE—DEFERRED, LOAD

Syntax

```
INTERFACE intf {DEFERRED [PUBLIC]} | LOAD.
```

Effect

Announces an interface.

Additions

- DEFERRED [PUBLIC]
  Deferred declaration of a local or global interface before its actual declaration in the program.
- LOAD
  Loads a global interface from the class library.

INTERFACE-POOL

Syntax

```
INTERFACE-POOL.
```

Effect

Initiates an interface pool.

INTERFACES

Syntax

```
INTERFACES intf
  { { [ABSTRACT METHODS meth1 meth2 ...]
      [FINAL METHODS meth1 meth2 ...] }
    | [ALL METHODS {ABSTRACT|FINAL}] }
  [DATA VALUES attr1 = val1 attr2 = val2 ...].
```

Effect

Includes an interface into the public visibility area of a class or into another interface.

Additions ab Release 6.10

- `ABSTRACT METHODS meth1 meth2 ...`
  Declares the specified instance methods `meth1 meth2 ...` as abstract during the implementation of the interface into a class.
- `FINAL METHODS meth1 meth2 ...`
  Declares the specified instance methods `meth1 meth2 ...` as final during the implementation of the interface into a class.
- `ALL METHODS {ABSTRACT|FINAL}`
  Declares all instance methods as abstract or final during the implementation of the interface into a class.
- `DATA VALUES attr1 = val1 attr2 = val2 ...`
  Assigns start values `val1 val2 ...` to instance attributes `attr1 attr2 ...` during the implementation of the interface into a class.

LEAVE

Syntax

```
LEAVE.
```

Release
Obsolete

Effect
Leaves a program depending on how the program was called.

LEAVE LIST-PROCESSING

Syntax

```
LEAVE LIST-PROCESSING.
```

Effect
Leaves the list processing and continues the processing with the PBO event of the dynpro, from which the list processor was called with `LEAVE TO LIST-PROCESSING`. Or, processing continues with the PBO event of the dynpro that was set with `AND RETURN TO SCREEN` while calling the list processor.

LEAVE PROGRAM

Syntax

```
LEAVE PROGRAM.
```

Effect
Leaves the current program and continues the processing, either after the calling point of the program or after the current call sequence, depending on how the program was called.

LEAVE SCREEN

Syntax

```
LEAVE { SCREEN | {TO SCREEN dynnr} }.
```

Effect
Leaves the current dynpro and continues the processing with the next dynpro.

Addition

- `TO SCREEN dynnr`
  Specifies the next dynpro in `dynnr`.

LEAVE TO LIST-PROCESSING

Syntax

```
LEAVE TO LIST-PROCESSING [AND RETURN TO SCREEN dynnr].
```

Effect

Calls list processing in the moment the current dynpro is left.

Addition

- `AND RETURN TO SCREEN dynnr`
  Specifies a dynpro `dynnr` to which to return upon completing the list processing.

LEAVE TO TRANSACTION

Syntax

```
LEAVE TO { {TRANSACTION ta} | {CURRENT TRANSACTION} }
         [AND SKIP FIRST SCREEN].
```

Effect

Calls a transaction without returning to the calling point.

Additions

- `TRANSACTION ta`
  Specifies a transaction code in `ta`.
- `AND SKIP FIRST SCREEN`
  Suspends the display of the initial screen.

Addition since Release 6.20

- `CURRENT TRANSACTION`
  Specifies the current transaction.

LOAD-OF-PROGRAM

Syntax

```
LOAD-OF-PROGRAM.
```

Effect

Initiates an event block whose event is triggered when the program is loaded into an internal session.

LOCAL

Syntax

```
LOCAL dobj.
```

Release

Obsolete

Effect

Saves the content of the data object dobj during a procedure in an internal cache.

L

log_exp

Syntax

```
{ {operand1 {=|EQ|<>|NE|>|GT|<|LT|>=|GE|<=|LE
            |CO|CN|CA|NA|CS|NS|CP|NP
            |BYTE-CO|BYTE-CN|BYTE-CA|BYTE-NA|BYTE-CS|BYTE-NS
            |O|Z|M} operand2}
| {operand [NOT] BETWEEN operand1 AND operand2}
| {<fs> IS [NOT] ASSIGNED}
| {ref IS [NOT] BOUND}
| {operand IS [NOT] INITIAL}
| {operand IS [NOT] REQUESTED}
| {operand IS [NOT] SUPPLIED}
| {[operand [NOT] IN] seltab} }
```

Effect

Logical expression to formulate a condition in certain statements. Logical expressions can be explicitly parenthesized with ( ), linked with AND and OR, and negated with NOT.

Additions

- =|EQ|<>|NE|>|GT|<|LT|>=|GE|<=|LE
  Relational operators for all data types.
- CO|CN|CA|NA|CS|NS|CP|NP
  Relational operators for character-type data types.
- O|Z M
  Relational operators for bit patterns.
- BETWEEN
  Determines an interval range.

- `IS ASSIGNED`
  Checks whether a memory area is assigned to a field symbol `<fs>`.
- `IS INITIAL`
  Determines whether an operand `operand` is initial.
- `IS SUPPLIED`
  Determines whether a formal parameter `operand` of a procedure is provided or requested.
- `[operand IN] seltab`
  Determines whether an operand `operand` meets the conditions of a selection table `seltab`.

Additions since Release 6.10

- `BYTE-CO|BYTE-CN|BYTE-CA|BYTE-NA|BYTE-CS|BYTE-NS`
  Relational operators for byte-type data types.
- `IS BOUND`
  Determines whether a reference variable `ref` is valid.
- `NOT`
  Use of `NOT` within logical expressions.

Obsolete addition

- `IS REQUESTED`
  Determines whether an output parameter `operand` of a procedure is requested.

LOG-POINT

Syntax

```
LOG-POINT ID group
          [SUBKEY sub]
          [FIELDS dobj1 dobj2 ...].
```

Release

7.0

Effect

Defines a logpoint to write a log entry.

Additions

- `ID group`
  Assigns the logpoint to a checkpoint group `group`, which controls its activation.

- `SUBKEY sub`
  Controls the summarization of the log via sub-key `sub`.
- `FIELDS dobj1 dobj2 ...`
  Writes the content of the data objects `dobj1 dobj2 ...` into the log.

LOOP

Syntax

```
LOOP.
  ...
ENDLOOP.
```

Effect

Reads out the extract dataset of a program in a loop. With each loop pass the content of the line being read out is assigned to the data objects that make up the field group defined with `INSERT FIELD-GROUP`.

LOOP AT dbtab

Syntax

```
LOOP AT dbtab [VERSION vers].
  ...
ENDLOOP.
```

Release

Obsolete

Effect

Reads out multiple rows from a database table `dbtab` in a loop. The content of the table work area `dbtab` is used as a search key.

Addition

- `VERSION vers`
  Specifies a different database table in `vers`.

LOOP AT itab

Syntax

```
LOOP AT itab { { INTO wa }
             | { ASSIGNING <fs> [CASTING] }
             | { REFERENCE INTO dref }
             | { TRANSPORTING NO FIELDS } }
             [FROM idx1] [TO idx2] [WHERE (log_exp)].
  ...
ENDLOOP.
```

Effect

Reads out an internal table itab in a loop.

Additions

- INTO wa
  Assigns the line that is read out to a work area wa.
- ASSIGNING <fs>
  Assigns the line that is read out to a field symbol <fs>.
- TRANSPORTING NO FIELDS
  No assignment of the line that is read.
- [FROM idx1] [TO idx2] [WHERE (*log_exp*)]
  Restricts the lines to be read out by indicating a lower and/or upper table index idx1 and idx2 or by indicating a condition *log_exp* (see log_exp entry).

Addition since Release 6.10

- REFERENCE INTO dref
  Assigns a reference to the read-out line to the reference variable dref.

Addition since Release 7.0

- CASTING
  Casts the line to the typing of the field symbol.

LOOP AT SCREEN

Syntax

```
LOOP AT SCREEN [INTO wa].
  ...
ENDLOOP.
```

Effect

Reads out the screen element properties of the current dynpro in a loop and assigns the results to the predefined structure `screen`.

Addition

- `INTO wa`
  Assigns these properties to a work area `wa` instead of the structure `screen`.

MAXIMUM

Syntax

```
MAXIMUM dobj.
```

Release

Obsolete

Effect

After the `MAXIMUM` statement the maximum value of `dobj` is determined with each `WRITE` statement for `dobj` and assigned to the data object `MAX_dobj`.

MESSAGE

Syntax

```
MESSAGE { tn
        | tn(id)
        | {ID mid TYPE mtype NUMBER num}
        | {oref TYPE mtype}
        | {text TYPE mtype} }
        { { [DISPLAY LIKE dtype]
            [RAISING exception] }
        | [INTO text] }
        [WITH dobj1 ... dobj4].
```

Effect

Sends a message.

Additions

- `tn`
  Message type `t`, message number `n`, message class from the `MESSAGE-ID` addition of the program initiation.

- `tn(id)`
  Message type `t`, message number `n`, message class `id`.
- `ID mid TYPE mtype NUMBER num`
  Message type from `mtype`, message number from `num`, message class from `mid`.
- `RAISING exception`
  Either sends the messages or triggers a non-class-based exception `exception` in a function module or method. An exception to which the return values are assigned at the calling point is triggered while another exception leads to sending the message.
- `INTO text`
  Returns the message text in `text`, and the message is not released.
- `WITH dobj1 ... dobj4`
  Replaces the placeholders &1 through &4 and & of the message text with the contents of `dobj1 ... dobj4`.

Additions since Release 6.10

- `text TYPE mtype`
  Message type from `mtype`, message text from `text`.
- `DISPLAY LIKE dtype`
  Displays the message in a dialog box and uses the icon of the message type specified in `dtype`.

Addition since Release 6.40

- `oref TYPE mtype`
  Message type from `mtype`, message number and message class from the interface IF_T100_MESSAGE implemented in the dynamic type of the object reference variable `oref`.

METHOD

Syntax

```
METHOD meth.
  ...
ENDMETHOD.
```

Effect

Implements a method `meth` in the implementation part of a class. A method is declared in the declaration part of the class and is implemented between `METHOD` and `ENDMETHOD`.

METHODS

Syntax

```
METHODS meth [ABSTRACT|FINAL]
             [FOR EVENT evt OF {class|intf}]
  [ IMPORTING {{VALUE(p1)|REFERENCE(p1)|p1} typing
                  [OPTIONAL|DEFAULT def1]
               {VALUE(p2)|REFERENCE(p2)|p2} typing
                   [OPTIONAL|DEFAULT def2]
               ... }
              [PREFERRED PARAMETER p] ]
  [ EXPORTING {{VALUE(p1)|REFERENCE(p1)|p1} typing
               {VALUE(p2)|REFERENCE(p2)|p2} typing
              ... } ]
  [ CHANGING  {{VALUE(p1)|REFERENCE(p1)|p1} typing
                  [OPTIONAL|DEFAULT def1]
               {VALUE(p2)|REFERENCE(p2)|p2} typing
                  [OPTIONAL|DEFAULT def2]
              ... } ]
  [ RETURNING {VALUE(r)} typing ]
  [ {RAISING|EXCEPTIONS} exc1 exc2 ... ].
```

Effect

Declares an instance method `meth` in a class or in an interface.

Additions

- `ABSTRACT`
  Declares an abstract method that cannot be implemented in the same class.
- `FINAL`
  Declares a final method that cannot be redefined in a subclass.
- `FOR EVENT evt OF {class|intf}`
  Declares an event-handler method that can handle the event `evt` of the class `class` or of the interface `intf`. Only input parameters are possible.
- `IMPORTING`
  Defines input parameters `p1 p2 ...`
- `EXPORTING`
  Defines output parameters `p1 p2 ...`
- `CHANGING`
  Defines input/output parameters `p1 p2 ...`

- `RETURNING`
  Declares a functional method with a completely typed return value `r`.
- `VALUE(p1) ... VALUE(p2) ...`
  Defines pass by value for a formal parameter.
- `REFERENCE(p1)|p1 ... REFERENCE(p2)|p2 ...`
  Defines pass by reference for a formal parameter.
- *`typing`*
  Types the formal parameters. See `typing` entry.
- `OPTIONAL|DEFAULT`
  Determines optional input or output parameters either without or with default parameters `def1 def2 ...`
- `PREFERRED PARAMETER p`
  Declares a parameter `p` out of exclusively optional input parameters as a preferred parameter.

Addition since Release 6.10

- `RAISING exc1 exc2 ...`
  Declares class-based exceptions `exc1 exc2 ...` that can be propagated from the method.

Obsolete addition

- `EXCEPTIONS exc1 exc2 ...`
  Defines non-class-based exceptions `exc1 exc2 ...`

METHODS—FOR TESTING

Syntax

```
METHODS meth FOR TESTING.
```

Release

6.40

Effect

Defines a testing method in a test class.

METHODS—REDEFINITION

Syntax

```
METHODS meth [FINAL] REDEFINITION.
```

Effect

Redefines an instance method of a superclass `meth` in the declaration part of a class. The method is re-implemented in the implementation part.

Addition

- `FINAL`
  Declares redefined method as final, so that it cannot be redefined again in a subclass.

MINIMUM

Syntax

```
MINIMUM dobj.
```

M

Release

Obsolete

Effect

After the `MINIMUM` statement, the minimum value of `dobj` is determined with each `WRITE` statement for `dobj` and assigned to the data object `MIN_dobj`.

MODIFY dbtab

Syntax

```
MODIFY {dbtab|(dbtab_syntax)} [CLIENT SPECIFIED]
       FROM { wa|{TABLE itab} }.
```

Effect

Inserts or overwrites rows in a database table.

Additions

- `{dbtab|(dbtab_syntax)}`
  Specifies the database table statically or dynamically.
- `CLIENT SPECIFIED`
  Switches off the automatic client handling.
- `FROM { wa|{TABLE itab} }`
  Specifies the rows to be inserted as work area `wa` or as lines of an internal table `itab`.

Addition since Release 6.10

▶ (dbtab_syntax)
In addition to flat character-type fields, strings and internal tables with a character-type line type can also be specified.

MODIFY itab

Syntax

```
MODIFY { { {TABLE itab}|{itab INDEX idx}
           FROM wa
           [TRANSPORTING comp1 comp2 ...]
           [{ASSIGNING <fs> [CASTING]}
           |{REFERENCE INTO dref}] }
       | {itab FROM wa TRANSPORTING comp1 comp2 ...
                   WHERE log_exp} }.
```

Effect

Modifies lines in internal tables.

Additions

▶ TABLE itab
Specifies a line to be modified by corresponding to the key values of the work area wa.

▶ itab INDEX idx
Specifies a line to be modified by indicating the table index idx.

▶ FROM wa
Specifies the new content in a work area wa.

▶ TRANSPORTING comp1 comp2 ...
Specifies the components comp1 comp2 ... to be modified.

▶ WHERE *log_exp*
Specifies the lines to be modified by a condition *log_exp* (see log_exp entry).

Additions since Release 6.10

▶ ASSIGNING <fs>
Assigns a modified single line to a field symbol <fs>.

▶ REFERENCE INTO dref
Assigns a reference to a modified single line to the reference variable dref.

Addition since Release 7.0

- `CASTING`
  Casts the line to the typing of the field symbol.

MODIFY LINE

Syntax

```
MODIFY { {LINE line [OF {PAGE page}|{CURRENT PAGE}]
                    [INDEX idx]}
       | {CURRENT LINE} }
       [LINE VALUE FROM wa]
       [FIELD VALUE dobj1 [FROM wa1] dobj2 [FROM wa2] ...]
       [LINE FORMAT ext_format_options]
       [FIELD FORMAT dobj1 ext_format_options1
                     dobj2 ext_format_options2 ...].
```

M

Effect

Overwrites a list line in the list buffer with the content of the system field `sy-lisel` and performs further modifications via the additions.

Additions

- `LINE line`
  Returns the number of lines to be modified in `line`.
- `OF {PAGE page}|{CURRENT PAGE}`
  Specifies the page in `page` or the uppermost page of the list on which a list event took place.
- `INDEX idx`
  Specifies the list index in `idx`. If nothing is specified, the list level is used at which a list event took place.
- `CURRENT LINE`
  Specifies the line in which a list event took place.
- `LINE VALUE FROM wa`
  Overwrites the entire list line with the content of `wa`.
- `FIELD VALUE dobj1 [FROM wa1] dobj2 [FROM wa2] ...`
  Overwrites the output areas of data objects `dobj1 dobj2 ...` specified in the list line with the current content of these objects or with the content of the data objects `wa1 wa2 ...`
- `LINE FORMAT ext_format_options`
  Formats the entire list line with the additions of the `FORMAT` statement.

- FIELD FORMAT dobj1 ext_format_options1 dobj2 ext_format_options2 ...
  Formats the output areas of data objects dobj1 dobj2 ... output in the list line with the additions of the FORMAT statement.

MODIFY SCREEN

Syntax

```
MODIFY SCREEN [FROM wa].
```

Effect

Overwrites the properties of the current screen element during LOOP AT SCREEN with the content of the predefined structure screen.

Addition

- FROM wa
  Uses a work area wa instead of the structure screen.

MODULE

Syntax

```
MODULE mod {OUTPUT|[INPUT]}.
  ...
ENDMODULE.
```

Effect

Defines a dialog module mod.

Additions

- OUTPUT
  Defines a dialog module for PBO.
- INPUT
  Defines a dialog module for PAI, POH or POV.

MOVE

Syntax

```
MOVE source {TO|?TO} destination.

destination {=|?=} source.
```

Effect

Assigns the content of `source` to `destination`. If a more general reference variable is assigned to a more specific one, `?TO` or `?=` must be used respectively.

MOVE-CORRESPONDING

Syntax

```
MOVE-CORRESPONDING struc1 TO struc2.
```

Effect

Assigns the components of a structure `struc1` to components having the same name of a structure `struc2`.

M

MOVE PERCENTAGE

Syntax

```
MOVE source TO destination PERCENTAGE perc [LEFT|RIGHT].
```

Release

Obsolete

Effect

Assigns the leading percentage `perc` of the character-type data object `source` to the data object `destination`.

Additions

- `LEFT`
  Fills `destination` left-aligned.
- `RIGHT`
  Fills `destination` right-aligned.

MULTIPLY

Syntax

```
MULTIPLY dobj1 BY dobj2.
```

Effect

Multiplies the content of `dobj1` by the content of `dobj2` and assigns the result to `dobj1`.

MULTIPLY-CORRESPONDING

Syntax

```
MULTIPLY-CORRESPONDING struc1 BY struc2.
```

Release

Obsolete

Effect

Multiplies the components of a structure `struc1` by components having the same name of a structure `struc2`.

NEW-LINE

Syntax

```
NEW-LINE [NO-SCROLLING|SCROLLING].
```

Effect

Creates a new line in a list.

Additions

- `NO-SCROLLING`
  The new line cannot be moved horizontally in the screen display.
- `SCROLLING`
  Undoes the `NO-SCROLLING` addition.

NEW-PAGE

Syntax

```
NEW-PAGE [WITH-TITLE|NO-TITLE]
         [WITH-HEADING|NO-HEADING]
         [LINE-COUNT page_lines]
         [LINE-SIZE width]
         [NO-TOPOFPAGE]
         [ { PRINT ON [NEW-SECTION]
                       PARAMETERS pri_params
                      [ARCHIVE PARAMETERS arc_params]
                       NO DIALOG }
         | { PRINT OFF } ].
```

Effect

Creates a new page in a list.

Additions

- `WITH-TITLE|NO-TITLE`
  Switches the standard heading on and off.
- `WITH-HEADING|NO-HEADING`
  Switches the column headings on and off.
- `LINE-COUNT page_lines`
  Determines the page length.
- `LINE-SIZE page_width`
  Determines the line width.
- `NO-TOPOFPAGE`
  Suppresses the `TOP-OF-PAGE` event.
- `PRINT ON`
  Diverts the output statements to a print list.
- `NEW-SECTION`
  Creates a new spool request with different print parameters.
- `PARAMETERS pri_params`
  Specifies the print parameters in a structure `pri_params` of the PRI_PARAMS type.
- `ARCHIVE PARAMETERS arc_params`
  Specifies the archiving parameters in a structure `arc_params` of the ARC_PARAMS type.
- `NO DIALOG`
  Suppresses the print dialog box.
- `PRINT OFF`
  Completes the current print list.

N

NEW-SECTION

Syntax

```
NEW-SECTION.
```

Release

Obsolete

Effect

Creates a new spool request during list creation.

NODES

Syntax

```
NODES node [TYPE type].
```

Effect

Declares an interface work area `node` for the data transfer of logical databases.

Addition

- `TYPE type`
  Specifies the data type `type` of the work area from a predefined list.

ON CHANGE OF

Syntax

```
ON CHANGE OF dobj [OR dobj1 [OR dobj2] ...].
  statement_block
ENDON.
```

Release

Obsolete

Effect

Defines a control structure with a statement block `statement_block`. The statement block is executed, if the data object `dobj` has changed since the last execution of the `ON CHANGE OF` statement.

Addition

- `OR dobj1 [OR dobj2] ...`
  The statement block is also executed, provided that the content of one of the data objects `dobj1 dobj2 ...` has changed.

OPEN CURSOR

Syntax

```
OPEN CURSOR [WITH HOLD] dbcur FOR
  SELECT [DISTINCT]
         { *
         | { {col1|aggregate( [DISTINCT] col1 )} [AS a1]
             {col2|aggregate( [DISTINCT] col2 )} [AS a2]
```

```
      ... }
    | (column_syntax) }
    FROM { { {dbtab [AS tabalias]}
           | { [(] {dbtab_left [AS tabalias_left]} | join
                  {[INNER] JOIN}|{LEFT [OUTER] JOIN}
                  {dbtab_right [AS tabalias_right]
                         ON sql_cond} [)]}
           | (dbtab_syntax) [AS tabalias] }
           [UP TO n ROWS]
           [CLIENT SPECIFIED]
           [BYPASSING BUFFER] }
    [[FOR ALL ENTRIES IN itab] WHERE sql_cond]
    [GROUP BY {col1 col2 ... }|(column_syntax)]
    [HAVING sql_cond]
    [ORDER BY { {PRIMARY KEY}
              |{{{col1|a1} [ASCENDING|DESCENDING]}
                {{col2|a2} [ASCENDING|DESCENDING]}
                ... }
              | (column_syntax) }].
```

O

Effect

Opens a database cursor for the selection defined with `SELECT`, and links a cursor variable `dbcur` to this cursor.

Additions

- `WITH HOLD`
  Leaves the database cursor open in the event of an explicitly triggered database commit or rollback.
- `DISTINCT`
  Excludes duplicate rows from the resulting set.
- `*`
  Reads all columns.
- `col1 col2 ...`
  Reads individual columns `col1 col2 ...`
- `aggregate( [DISTINCT] col1 ) aggregate( [DISTINCT] col2 ) ...`
  Evaluates aggregate functions `aggregate` (see `aggregate` entry) for columns `col1 col2 ...`; duplicate arguments can be excluded.
- `AS a1, AS a2 ...`
  Defines alternative column names `a1 a2 ...`

- (column_syntax)
  Specifies the columns as content of column_syntax.
- FROM dbtab [AS tabalias]
  Specifies a database table dbtab.
- FROM [(] {dbtab_left [AS tabalias_left]} | join
  {[INNER] JOIN}|{LEFT [OUTER] JOIN}
  {dbtab_right [AS tabalias_right] ON *sql_cond*} [)]
  Combines a database table dbtab_left or a join expression join with a database table dbtab_right to create a join expression. Inner and outer joins can be built with join conditions *sql_cond* that are—with a few restrictions—identical to the WHERE conditions.
- (dbtab_syntax)
  Specifies the database tables as content of source_syntax.
- AS tabalias
  Defines an alternative table name tabalias.
- UP TO n ROWS
  Limits the number of rows read to n.
- CLIENT SPECIFIED
  Switches off the automatic client handling.
- BYPASSING BUFFER
  Bypasses the SAP buffering.
- FOR ALL ENTRIES IN itab
  Enables a logical condition on all lines of an internal table itab after WHERE.
- WHERE *sql_cond*
  Restricts the resulting set by a condition *sql_cond* (see sql_cond entry). The condition can consist of various logical expressions.
- GROUP BY { col1 col2 ... | (column_syntax) }
  Summarizes groups of rows with the same content in the columns col1 col2 ... to create a single row of the resulting set. The columns can be specified dynamically in column_syntax.
- HAVING *sql_cond*
  Restricts the summarized rows into groups in the resulting set by a condition *sql_cond* (see sql_cond entry).
- ORDER BY
  {PRIMARY KEY}|{{{col1|a1} [ASCENDING|DESCENDING]}
  {{col2|a2} [ASCENDING|DESCENDING]} ...}|(column_syntax)
  Sorts the resulting set according to the primary key, statically spe-

cified columns col1 col2 ... or a1 a2 ..., or according to columns dynamically specified in column_syntax; the sorting direction can be indicated for each column.

Additions since Release 6.10

- (dbtab_syntax)
  In addition to flat character-type fields, strings and internal tables with a character-type line type can also be specified. Specification of named data objects. Use in DELETE and UPDATE.
- (column_syntax)
  In addition to internal tables with flat character-type line type, character-type fields and internal tables with a deep character type line type can also be specified.

OPEN DATASET

O

Syntax

```
OPEN DATASET dset
  FOR { INPUT | OUTPUT | APPENDING | UPDATE }
  IN { { BINARY MODE }
     | { TEXT MODE
           ENCODING { DEFAULT
                    | {UTF-8 [SKIPPING|WITH BYTE-ORDER MARK]}
                    | NON-UNICODE }
           [WITH {NATIVE|SMART|UNIX|WINDOWS} LINEFEED] }
     | { LEGACY BINARY MODE
           [{BIG|LITTLE} ENDIAN]
           [CODE PAGE cp] }
     | { LEGACY TEXT MODE
           [{BIG|LITTLE} ENDIAN]
           [CODE PAGE cp]
           [WITH {NATIVE|SMART|UNIX|WINDOWS} LINEFEED] } }
   [AT POSITION pos]
   [TYPE attr]
   [FILTER opcom]
   [MESSAGE msg]
   [IGNORING CONVERSION ERRORS]
   [REPLACEMENT CHARACTER rc].
```

Effect

Opens the file specified in dset on the application server.

Additions

- `FOR { INPUT | OUTPUT | APPENDING }`
  Opens the file for reading, writing or appending.
- `AT POSITION pos`
  Places the file pointer in the position specified in `pos`.
- `TYPE attr`
  Either sets OS-dependent parameters of the file or controls the end-of-line mark of a text file (prior to Release 7.0).
- `FILTER opcom`
  Passes a statement to the operating system.
- `MESSAGE msg`
  Returns the corresponding OS message in `msg` in the case of an error.

Additions since Release 6.10

- `FOR UPDATE`
  Opens the file for changing.
- `IN [LEGACY] { BINARY | TEXT } MODE`
  Opens the file in normal binary or text mode or in the legacy-binary or text mode respectively.
- `ENCODING {DEFAULT|UTF-8|NON-UNICODE}`
  Determines in which character display mode the content of the file will be handled:
  - `DEFAULT`—UTF-8 in Unicode systems, no conversion in non-Unicode systems.
  - `UTF-8`—UTF-8.
  - `NON-UNICODE`—Code page according to non-Unicode text environment in Unicode systems; no conversion in non-Unicode systems.
- `{BIG|LITTLE} ENDIAN`
  Determines in which endian numerical data objects in the file will be handled.
- `CODE PAGE cp`
  Determines that character-type data objects in the file are treated according to the code page specified in `cp`.
- `IGNORING CONVERSION ERRORS`
  Suppresses an exception in the event of a conversion error.

- `REPLACEMENT CHARACTER rc`
  Specifies a replacement character for non-convertible characters in `rc`. If nothing is specified, "#" will be used by default.

Additions since Release 7.0

- `WITH {NATIVE|SMART|UNIX|WINDOWS} LINEFEED`
  Determines the end-of-line mark for text files.
- `SKIPPING|WITH BYTE-ORDER MARK`
  Controls the handling of the byte-order mark in UTF-8 text files.

OVERLAY

Syntax

```
OVERLAY text1 WITH text2 [ONLY pattern].
```

Effect

Replaces blanks in `text1` with the characters from the same positions in `text2`.

P

Addition

- `ONLY pattern`
  Replaces all characters contained in the data object `pattern`, not only the blanks.

PACK

Syntax

```
PACK source TO destination.
```

Release

Obsolete

Effect

Packs the numerical content of a character-type data object `source` into the digits of a packed number `destination`.

PARAMETERS

Syntax

```
PARAMETERS { {para[(len)]} | {para [LENGTH len]} }
           [ {TYPE type [DECIMALS dec]}
```

```
| {LIKE dobj}
| {LIKE (name)} ]
[ {[OBLIGATORY|NO-DISPLAY] [VISIBLE LENGTH vlen]}
| {AS CHECKBOX [USER-COMMAND fcode]}
| {RADIOBUTTON GROUP group [USER-COMMAND fcode]}
| {AS LISTBOX VISIBLE LENGTH vlen
     [USER-COMMAND fcode] [OBLIGATORY]} ]
[MODIF ID modid]
[DEFAULT val]
[LOWER CASE]
[MATCHCODE OBJECT search_help]
[MEMORY ID pid]
[VALUE CHECK]
[FOR {TABLE|NODE} node
   [HELP-REQUEST]
   [VALUE-REQUEST]
   [AS SEARCH PATTERN]].
```

Effect

Declares a parameter `para` and creates a corresponding input field in the current selection screen.

Additions

- `(len)`
  Determines the length when referring to generic built-in ABAP types.
- `TYPE type [DECIMALS dec]`
  Specifies the data type `type` directly and determines the number of fractional portions.
- `LIKE dobj`
  Specifies the data type by referring to a data object `dobj`.
- `LIKE (name)`
  Fixes the data type to `c`, length 132, and displays the input field according to the type that is dynamically specified in `name`.
- `OBLIGATORY`
  Defines the input field as an obligatory field.
- `NO-DISPLAY`
  No input field is created in the selection screen.
- `VISIBLE LENGTH vlen`
  Determines the visible length of the input field to be `vlen`.

- `AS CHECKBOX`
  Creates the input field as a checkbox.
- `RADIOBUTTON GROUP group`
  Creates the input field as a radio button of the radio button group `group`.
- `AS LISTBOX`
  Creates a drop-down list box for the input field.
- `USER-COMMAND fcode`
  Links the input field to a function code.
- `MODIF ID modid`
  Assigns the input field to the modification group `modid`.
- `DEFAULT val`
  Determines a start value `val` for the content of the parameter.
- `LOWER CASE`
  Avoids converting the content of character-type fields into upper case letters during the transfer between input field and data object.
- `MATCHCODE OBJECT search_help`
  Links the input field to a search help `search_help` from the ABAP dictionary.
- `MEMORY ID pid`
  Links the input field to the SPA/GPA parameter `pid` in the SAP memory.
- `VALUE CHECK`
  Checks the entry against type-specific default values from the ABAP dictionary.
- `FOR {TABLE|NODE} node`
  Assigns parameters in a logical database to a node `node` of the corresponding structure.
- `[HELP-REQUEST] [VALUE-REQUEST]`
  Enables self-defined field and input helps for the input field in logical databases.
- `AS SEARCH PATTERN`
  Enables the evaluation of a search help in logical databases.

Addition since Release 6.10

- `LENGTH len`
  Determines the length when referring to generic built-in ABAP types.

P

Addition since Release 6.20

- `USER-COMMAND fcode`
  Can be used in combination with `LISTBOX`.

PERFORM

Syntax

```
PERFORM { { { subr
            | {subr|(sname) IN PROGRAM [prog|(pname)]
                                       [IF FOUND]}
            | {n OF subr1 subr2 ...}
            | {subr(prog) [IF FOUND]} }
            [TABLES itab1 itab2 ...]
            [USING a1 a2 ...]
            [CHANGING a1 a2 ...] }
        | { ON { {COMMIT [LEVEL idx]}
               | ROLLBACK } } }.
```

Effect

Calls a subroutine.

Additions

- `subr`
  Specifies a subroutine `subr` of the same program.
- `subr|(sname) IN PROGRAM [prog|(pname)]`
  Specifies a subroutine of any program statically or dynamically.
- `n OF subr1 subr2 ...`
  Specifies a subroutine `n` from a list of subroutines.
- `IF FOUND`
  Suppresses an exception, when the subroutine is not found.
- `TABLES itab1 itab2 ...`
  Assigns internal tables `itab1 itab2 ...` to the table parameters of the same position.
- `USING a1 a2 ...`
  Assigns actual parameters `a1 a2 ...` to the formal parameters of the same position.
- `CHANGING a1 a2 ...`
  Assigns actual parameters `a1 a2 ...` to the formal parameters of the same position.

▶ ON COMMIT [LEVEL idx]
Registers the subroutine for execution on COMMIT WORK, where the execution sequence can be controlled with LEVEL.

▶ ON ROLLBACK
Registers the subroutine for execution on ROLLBACK WORK.

Obsolete addition

▶ subr(prog)
Specifies statically a subroutine of a program prog.

POSITION

Syntax

```
POSITION pos.
```

Effect

Places the list cursor to the position in the current list line which is specified in pos.

P

PRINT-CONTROL

Syntax

```
PRINT-CONTROL { { formats|{FUNCTION code}
                  [LINE line] [POSITION col] }
              | { INDEX-LINE index_line } }.
```

Effect

Specifies a print format or creates index entries for the list archiving.

Additions

▶ formats
Predefined print formats for print-control codes.

▶ FUNCTION code
Specifies print-control codes directly in code.

▶ [LINE line] [POSITION col]
Sets the print format to begin at the list line specified in line and at the position specified in col.

▶ INDEX-LINE index_line
Inserts the content of index_line as an index line into the current print list.

PROGRAM

Syntax

```
PROGRAM prog [NO STANDARD PAGE HEADING]
             [LINE-SIZE width]
             [LINE-COUNT page_lines[(footer_lines)]]
             [MESSAGE-ID mid].
```

Effect

Initiates a program prog.

Additions

- NO STANDARD PAGE HEADING
  Suppresses the output of the standard page header.
- LINE-SIZE width
  Sets the line width of the program's lists to width characters.
- LINE-COUNT page_lines[(footer_lines)]
  Sets the page length of the program's basic list to page_lines lines and reserves footer_lines footer lines.
- MESSAGE-ID mid
  Determines a message class mid for short forms of MESSAGE.

PROVIDE

Syntax

```
PROVIDE FIELDS {*|{comp1 comp2 ...}}
               FROM itab1 INTO wa1 VALID flag1
               BOUNDS intliml1 AND intlimu1
               [WHERE log_exp1]
        FIELDS {*|{comp1 comp2 ...}}
               FROM itab2 INTO wa2 VALID flag2
               BOUNDS intliml2 AND intlimu2
               [WHERE log_exp2]
               ...
        BETWEEN extliml AND extlimu
        [INCLUDING GAPS].
  ...
ENDPROVIDE.
```

Effect

Evaluates a join of specific internal tables in a loop. Overlapping value intervals in the respective internal tables are the basis of the join.

Additions

- `{*|(comp1 comp2 ...)}`
  Specifies the columns to be read.
- `FROM itab1 ... FROM itab2 ...`
  Specifies the internal tables involved.
- `BETWEEN extliml AND extlimu`
  Specifies an outer interval.

Additions since Release 6.20

- `FIELDS`
  Distinguishes between the statement and its obsolete short form (see below).
- `INTO wa1 ... INTO wa2 ...`
  Specifies work areas for the results.
- `VALID flag1 ... VALID flag2 ...`
  Notifies whether or not the intervals of the internal tables overlap in the current loop.
- `BOUNDS intliml1 AND intlimu1, ...`
  Specifies two specific columns of each internal table whose values must be interpretable as boundaries of closed intervals.
- `WHERE` *`log_exp1`* `...` `WHERE` *`log_exp2`* `...`
  Specifies a condition via a logical expression *`log_exp`* (see `log_exp` entry).
- `INCLUDING GAPS`
  Defines that the loop is passed even for non-overlapping intervals.

Obsolete short form

- Outside classes `PROVIDE` can still be used in an obsolete short form without the additions that are available since Release 6.20.

PUT

Syntax

```
PUT { node | <node> }.
```

Effect

Triggers the `GET node` event in a logical database, if data is available in the table work area of the node `node`. For node type A, the field symbol `<node>` is specified and assigned to a data object of the data type requested in the `NODES` statement in the executable program that is linked to it.

RAISE

Syntax

```
RAISE exception.
```

Release

Obsolete since Release 6.10

Effect

Triggers a non-class-based exception in a function module or in a method.

RAISE EVENT

Syntax

```
RAISE EVENT evt [EXPORTING p1 = a1 p2 = a2 ...].
```

Effect

Triggers an event in a method.

Addition

- `EXPORTING p1 = a1 p2 = a2 ...`
  Assings actual parameters `a1 a2 ...` to the input parameters `p1 p2 ...` of the event handlers.

RAISE EXCEPTION

Syntax

```
RAISE EXCEPTION { {TYPE cx_class
                     [EXPORTING p1 = a1 p2 = a2 ...]}
                | oref }.
```

Release

6.10

Effect

Triggers a class-based exception.

Additions

- `TYPE cx_class [EXPORTING p1 = a1 p2 = a2 ...]`
  Specifies the exception class and assigns actual parameters `a1 a2 ...` to the input parameters `p1 p2 ...` of the constructor.
- `oref`
  Uses an existing exception object which is addressed by `oref`.

RANGES

Syntax

```
RANGES rtab FOR dobj [OCCURS n].
```

Release

Obsolete

Effect

Creates a ranges table with a header line and the line type of a selection table.

Addition

- `OCCURS n`
  Specifies the initial memory allocation `n`.

READ DATASET

Syntax

```
READ DATASET dset INTO dobj [MAXIMUM LENGTH mlen]
                            [[ACTUAL] LENGTH alen].
```

Effect

Reads data from the file specified in `dset` into the data object `dobj`.

Addition

- `LENGTH alen`
  Returns the number of characters or bytes read from the file in `alen`.

Additions since Release 6.10

- `MAXIMUM LENGTH mlen`
  Limits the number of characters or bytes to be read from the file to `mlen`.
- `ACTUAL`
  Helps differentiate the addition `LENGTH` from `MAXIMUM LENGTH`.

READ LINE

Syntax

```
READ { {LINE line [{OF PAGE page}|{OF CURRENT PAGE}]
                  [INDEX idx]}
     | {CURRENT LINE} }
     [LINE VALUE INTO wa]
     [FIELD VALUE dobj1 [INTO wa1] dobj2 [INTO wa2] ...].
```

Effect

Reads a list line in the list buffer and assigns the content to `sy-lisel`.

Additions

- `LINE line`
  Specifies the line to be read in `line`.
- `OF {PAGE page}|{CURRENT PAGE}`
  Specifies the page in `page` or the uppermost page of the list on which a list event took place.
- `INDEX idx`
  Specifies the list index in `idx`. If nothing is specified, the list level is used at which a list event took place.
- `CURRENT LINE`
  Specifies the line in which a list event took place.
- `LINE VALUE INTO wa`
  Assigns the content of the list line to the work area `wa`.
- `FIELD VALUE dobj1 [INTO wa1] dobj2 [INTO wa2] ...`
  Assigns the output areas of data objects `dobj1 dobj2 ...` output in the list line to these objects or to the data objects `wa1 wa2 ...`

READ REPORT

Syntax

```
READ REPORT prog INTO itab [MAXIMUM WIDTH INTO wid].
```

Effect

Reads the source code of the ABAP program `prog` into the internal table `itab`.

Addition since Release 6.10

- `MAXIMUM WIDTH INTO wid`
  Returns the number of characters of the longest source code line that was read in `wid`.

READ TABLE dbtab

Syntax

```
READ TABLE dbtab [WITH KEY key]
                 [SEARCH {FKEQ|FKGE|GKEQ|GKGE}]
                 [VERSION vers].
```

Release

Obsolete

Effect

Reads a single row from a database table `dbtab`.

Additions

- `WITH KEY key`
  Determines the search key via the content of the data object `key`. Alternatively the content of the table work area `dbtab` is used as a search key.
- `SEARCH {FKEQ|FKGE|GKEQ|GKGE}`
  Determines the search mode in the database table.
- `VERSION vers`
  Specifies a different database table in `vers`.

READ TABLE itab

Syntax

```
READ TABLE itab
          { {{FROM wa}
```

R

```
        |{WITH TABLE KEY {comp_name1|(name1)} = dobj1
                         {comp_name2|(name2)} = dobj2
                         ...}
        | {WITH KEY comp1 = dobj1 comp2 = dobj2 ...
            [BINARY SEARCH]}
        | {INDEX idx} }
        | {WITH KEY dobj}
        | {WITH KEY = dobj [BINARY SEARCH]} }
      { {INTO wa
          [COMPARING { {comp1 comp2 ...}
                     |{ALL FIELDS}
                     |{NO FIELDS} }]
          [TRANSPORTING { {comp1 comp2 ...}
                        |{ALL FIELDS} }]}
      | {ASSIGNING <fs> [CASTING]}
      | {REFERENCE INTO dref}
      | {TRANSPORTING NO FIELDS} }.
```

Effect

Reads a single line from an internal table `itab`.

Additions

- `FROM wa`
  Specifies the line to be read by corresponding to the key values of a work area `wa`.
- `WITH TABLE KEY {comp_name1|(name1)} = dobj1 {comp_name2|(name2)} = dobj2 ...`
  Specifies the line to be read by statically or dynamically indicating the table key components.
- `WITH KEY comp1 = dobj1 comp2 = dobj2 ... [BINARY SEARCH]`
  Specifies the line to be read by indicating any components `comp1 comp2 ...`, whereby standard tables that are sorted appropriately are searched binarily with `BINARY SEARCH`.
- `INDEX idx`
  Specifies the line to be read by indicating the table index `idx`.
- `INTO wa`
  Assigns the line that is read out to a work area `wa`.
- `COMPARING { {comp1 comp2 ...}|{ALL FIELDS}|{NO FIELDS} }`
  Compares the components `comp1 comp2 ...`, all components, or no components of a line that was found with the corresponding

components of the work area. The command sets sy-subrc accordingly.

- TRANSPORTING { {comp1 comp2 ...}|{ALL FIELDS} }
  Assigns the specified components comp1 comp2 ... or all components of the line that was found to the work area wa.
- ASSIGNING <fs>
  Assigns the line that is read out to a field symbol <fs>.
- TRANSPORTING NO FIELDS
  The line that was read out is not assigned.

Addition since Release 6.10

- REFERENCE INTO dref
  Assigns a reference to the read-out line to the reference variable dref.

Addition since Release 7.0

- CASTING
  Casts the line to the typing of the field symbol.

Obsolete Additions

- WITH KEY dobj
  Reads the first line whose left-sided content corresponds to the content of the data object dobj; at the same time the table line is cast to the type of dobj.
- WITH KEY = dobj [BINARY SEARCH]
  Reads the first line whose entire content corresponds to the content of the data object dobj. Tables that are sorted accordingly are searched in binary mode with BINARY SEARCH.

READ TEXTPOOL

Syntax

```
READ TEXTPOOL prog INTO itab LANGUAGE lang.
```

Effect

Reads the text elements of the language specified in lang and of the program specified in prog into the internal table itab of the TEXTPOOL type.

RECEIVE

Syntax

```
RECEIVE RESULTS FROM FUNCTION func
   [IMPORTING p1 = a1 p2 = a2 ...]
   [TABLES t1 = itab1 t2 = itab2 ...]
   [EXCEPTIONS [exc1 = n1 exc2 = n2 ...]
               [system_failure = ns [MESSAGE smess]]
               [communication_failure = nc [MESSAGE cmess]]
               [OTHERS = n_o]]
   [KEEPING TASK].
```

Effect

Receives the result of an asynchronous RFC in a callback routine.

Additions

- `IMPORTING p1 = a1 p2 = a2 ...`
  Assigns output parameters `p1 p2 ...` to actual parameters `a1 a2 ...`
- `TABLES t1 = itab1 t2 = itab2 ...`
  Assigns internal tables `itab1 itab2 ...` to table parameters `t1 t2 ...`
- `EXCEPTIONS`
  Enables the handling of non-class-based exceptions:
  - `exc1 = n1 exc2 = n2`—Assigns numbers `n1 n2 ...` for the return value `sy-subrc` to the classical exceptions `exc1 exc2 ...`
  - `system_failure`, `communication_failure`—Handles special RFC exceptions and adopts the first line of the short dump after `smess` or `cmess`.
  - `OTHERS = n_o`—Assigns a number `n_o` for the return value `sy-subrc` to all exceptions not explicitly named.
- `KEEPING TASK`
  Prevents the RFC connection from being closed after the results have been transferred.

REFRESH

Syntax

```
REFRESH itab.
```

Effect
Deletes all lines of an internal table itab.

REFRESH CONTROL

Syntax

```
REFRESH CONTROL contrl FROM SCREEN dynnr.
```

Effect
Assigns the values predefined in dynpro dynnr to the components of the structure contrl defined for a table control with CONTROLS.

REFRESH—FROM

Syntax

```
REFRESH itab FROM TABLE dbtab.
```

R

Release
Obsolete

Effect
Deletes all lines of an internal table itab and fills the table with rows from the database dbtab. The content of the table work area dbtab is used as a search key.

REJECT

Syntax

```
REJECT [node].
```

Effect
Leaves the current GET event block of an executable program.

Addition
- node

  The logical database reads the next data record of the node node.

REPLACE

Syntax

```
REPLACE { { [{FIRST OCCURRENCE}|{ALL OCCURRENCES OF}]
            {[SUBSTRING] sub_string} | {REGEX regex} IN
            { {[SECTION [OFFSET off] [LENGTH len] OF] dobj}
            | {TABLE itab [FROM lin1 [OFFSET off1]]
                          [TO   lin2 [OFFSET off2]]} }
            WITH new
            [IN {BYTE|CHARACTER} MODE]
            [{RESPECTING|IGNORING} CASE]
            [REPLACEMENT COUNT rcnt]
            { {[REPLACEMENT OFFSET roff]
               [REPLACEMENT LENGTH rlen]
               [REPLACEMENT LINE   rlin]}
            | [RESULTS result_tab|result_wa] } }
        | { SECTION [OFFSET off] [LENGTH len] OF dobj
            WITH new
            [IN {BYTE|CHARACTER} MODE] } }.
```

Release

6.10

Effect

Replaces byte strings or characters strings in a byte or character like data object `dobj` or in an internal table `itab` with the contents of `new`. The characters or bytes to be replaced are identified by means of a search for substrings or regular expressions, or by directly specifying the offset and length.

Additions

- `sub_string`
  Specifies a substring to be searched and replaced.
- `SECTION [OFFSET off] [LENGTH len] OF`
  Specifies a section of `dobj` beginning at the offset specified in `off` with the length specified in `len`. This can be either the section to be searched in or the one to be replaced.
- `{FIRST OCCURRENCE}|{ALL OCCURRENCES OF}`
  Determines whether the first occurrence or all occurrences are to be replaced.
- `IN {BYTE|CHARACTER} MODE`
  Determines byte or character string processing.

- {RESPECTING|IGNORING} CASE
  Determines whether uppercase and lowercase letters are considered during the search.
- REPLACEMENT COUNT rcnt
  Returns the number of replacements in rcnt.
- REPLACEMENT OFFSET roff
  Returns the offset of the last replacement in roff.
- REPLACEMENT LENGTH rlen
  Returns the length of the last replacement in rlen.

Additions since Release 7.0

- {[SUBSTRING] sub_string} | {REGEX regex}
  Determines whether a substring substring or a regular expression regex is searched for or replaced (see pages 187–189).
- TABLE itab [FROM lin1 [OFFSET off1]] [TO lin2 [OFFSET off2]]
  Makes replacements in an internal table itab where the search area is restricted to the section that begins with the line specified in lin1 and the offset specified in off1 and continues up to the line specified in lin2 and the offset specified in off2.
- REPLACEMENT LINE rlin
  Returns the table line of the last replacement in rlin.
- RESULTS result_tab|result_wa
  Returns the properties of all replacements or of the last replacement in an internal table result_tab or in a structure result_wa of the MATCH_RESULTS type.

REPLACE sub_string WITH

Syntax

```
REPLACE sub_string WITH new INTO dobj
        [IN {BYTE|CHARACTER} MODE]
        [LENGTH len].
```

Release

Obsolete since Release 6.10

Effect

Searches for a byte or character string sub_string in the variable dobj and replaces the string with the contents of new.

Addition

- `LENGTH len`
  Uses only the first `len` bytes or characters of `sub_string` for the search.

Addition since Release 6.10

- `IN {BYTE|CHARACTER} MODE`
  Determines byte or character string processing.

REPORT

Syntax

```
REPORT rep [NO STANDARD PAGE HEADING]
           [LINE-SIZE width]
           [LINE-COUNT page_lines[(footer_lines)]]
           [MESSAGE-ID mid]
           [DEFINING DATABASE ldb].
```

Effect

Initiates an executable program `rep`.

Additions

- `NO STANDARD PAGE HEADING`
  Suppresses the output of the standard page header.
- `LINE-SIZE width`
  Sets the line width of the program's lists to `width` characters.
- `LINE-COUNT page_lines[(footer_lines)]`
  Sets the page length of the program's basic list to `page_lines` lines and reserves `footer_lines` footer lines.
- `MESSAGE-ID mid`
  Determines a message class `mid` for short forms of `MESSAGE`.
- `DEFINING DATABASE ldb`
  Does not initiate an executable program, but rather the database program of the logical database `ldb`.

RESERVE

Syntax

```
RESERVE n LINES.
```

Effect
Creates a page break in a list, if on the current page of the list there are no longer n lines available.

RETURN

Syntax

```
RETURN.
```

Release
6.10

Effect
Leaves the current processing block.

ROLLBACK

Syntax

```
ROLLBACK WORK.
```

S

Effect
Terminates an SAP LUW. The subroutines registered with PERFORM ON ROLLBACK and the update function modules registered with PERFORM ON COMMIT or CALL FUNCTION IN UPDATE TASK are discarded.

SCROLL

Syntax

```
SCROLL LIST [ { TO COLUMN col }
            | { {LEFT|RIGHT} [BY n PLACES] } ]
            [ { TO { {FIRST PAGE}
                   | {LAST PAGE}
                   | {PAGE pag} }
                   [LINE lin] }
              | { {FORWARD|BACKWARD} [n PAGES] } ]
            [INDEX idx].
```

Effect
Moves the display area of a list that is stored in the list buffer.

Additions

- TO COLUMN col
  Moves horizontally until column col is reached.
- {LEFT|RIGHT} [BY n PLACES]
  Moves to the left or right either by the width of the line or by n places.
- TO { {FIRST PAGE} | {LAST PAGE} | {PAGE pag} [LINE lin] }
  Moves vertically to the first page, the last page or the one specified in pag; the uppermost line lin can be specified.
- {FORWARD|BACKWARD} [n PAGES]
  Moves upwards or downwards by one page or by pag pages.
- INDEX idx
  Specifies the list index in idx. If nothing is specified, the list level is used at which a list event took place.

SEARCH

Syntax

```
SEARCH dobj|itab FOR pattern
       [IN {BYTE|CHARACTER} MODE]
       [STARTING AT p1] [ENDING AT p2]
       [ABBREVIATED]
       [AND MARK].
```

Release

Partly obsolete since Release 6.10; completely obsolete since Release 7.0.

Effect

Searches the data object dobj or the internal table itab for the search pattern specified in pattern.

Additions

- [STARTING AT p1] [ENDING AT p2]
  Restricts the search to the sub-area between positions p1 and p2 of dobj or to the lines between p1 and p2 in itab.
- ABBREVIATED
  Permits the specification of an abbreviated pattern in pattern.
- AND MARK
  Converts a pattern that was found into uppercase letters in dobj or itab respectively.

Addition since Release 6.10

- IN {BYTE|CHARACTER} MODE
  Determines byte or character string processing.

SELECT

Syntax

```
SELECT { { SINGLE [FOR UPDATE] }
       | { [DISTINCT] { }        } }
       { *
       | { {col1|aggregate( [DISTINCT] col1 )} [AS a1]
           {col2|aggregate( [DISTINCT] col2 )} [AS a2]   ... }
       | (column_syntax) }
       FROM { { {dbtab [AS tabalias]}
              | { [(] {dbtab_left [AS tabalias_left]} | join
                      {[INNER] JOIN}|{LEFT [OUTER] JOIN}
                      {dbtab_right [AS tabalias_right]
                                   ON sql_cond} [)]}
              | (dbtab_syntax) [AS tabalias] }
              [UP TO n ROWS]
              [CLIENT SPECIFIED]
              [BYPASSING BUFFER] }
       { { INTO {[CORRESPONDING FIELDS OF] wa}
                |(dobj1, dobj2, ...) }
       | { INTO|APPENDING [CORRESPONDING FIELDS OF]
                         TABLE itab
                         [PACKAGE SIZE n] } }
       [[FOR ALL ENTRIES IN itab] WHERE sql_cond]
       [GROUP BY {col1 col2 ... }|(column_syntax)]
       [HAVING sql_cond]
       [ORDER BY { {PRIMARY KEY}
                 |{{{col1|a1} [ASCENDING|DESCENDING]}
                   {{col2|a2} [ASCENDING|DESCENDING]}
                   ... }
                 | (column_syntax) }].
  ...
[ENDSELECT.].
```

Effect

Reads data from one or more database tables into data objects. If the resulting set is not assigned completely all at once, a loop is initiated which has to be completed with ENDSELECT; the results will be available in the target fields of the loop.

Additions

- SINGLE|{ }
  Defines a resulting set in a single row or in multiple rows.
- FOR UPDATE
  Activates write protection for the database.
- DISTINCT
  Excludes duplicate rows from the resulting set.
- *
  Reads all columns.
- col1 ... col2 ...
  Reads individual columns col1 col2 ...
- *aggregate*([DISTINCT] col1) *aggregate*([DISTINCT] col2) ...
  Evaluates aggregate functions *aggregate* (see aggregate entry) for columns col1 col2 ...; duplicate arguments can be excluded.
- AS a1 ... AS a2 ...
  Defines alternative column names a1 a2 ...
- (column_syntax)
  Specifies the columns as content of column_syntax.
- FROM dbtab [AS tabalias]
  Specifies a database table dbtab.
- FROM [(] {dbtab_left [AS tabalias_left]} | join
  {[INNER] JOIN}|{LEFT [OUTER] JOIN}
  {dbtab_right [AS tabalias_right] ON *sql_cond*} [)]
  Combines a database table dbtab_left or a join expression join with a database table dbtab_right to a join expression. Inner and outer joins can be built with join conditions *sql_cond* that are—with a few restrictions—identical to the WHERE conditions.
- (dbtab_syntax)
  Specifies the database tables as content of source_syntax.
- AS tabalias
  Defines an alternative table name tabalias.
- UP TO n ROWS
  Limits the number of rows read to n.
- CLIENT SPECIFIED
  Switches off the automatic client handling.

- `BYPASSING BUFFER`
  Bypasses the SAP buffering.
- `INTO wa|(dobj1, dobj2 ...)`
  Specifies a work area `wa` or a list of data objects `dobj1 dobj2 ...` as target fields.
- `INTO|APPENDING TABLE itab [PACKAGE SIZE n]`
  Specifies an internal table `itab` as target area. The resulting set is written completely or in packages into the table or appended to it.
- `CORRESPONDING FIELDS OF`
  Transports only those columns for which target fields with the same name exist.
- `FOR ALL ENTRIES IN itab`
  Enables a logical condition on all lines of an internal table `itab` after `WHERE`.
- `WHERE` *`sql_cond`*
  Restricts the resulting set by a condition *`sql_cond`* (see `sql_cond` entry). The condition can consist of various logical expressions.
- `GROUP BY { col1 col2 ... | (column_syntax) }`
  Condenses groups of rows with the same content in the columns `col1 col2 ...` into a single row of the resulting set. The columns can be specified dynamically in `column_syntax`.
- `HAVING` *`sql_cond`*
  Restricts the rows that were condensed into groups in the resulting set by a condition *`sql_cond`* (see `sql_cond` entry).
- `ORDER BY`
  `{PRIMARY KEY}|{{{col1|a1} [ASCENDING|DESCENDING]}`
  `{{col2|a2} [ASCENDING|DESCENDING]} ...}|(column_syntax)`
  Sorts the resulting set according to the primary key, statically specified columns `col1 col2 ...` or `a1 a2 ...`, or according to columns dynamically specified in `column_syntax`. The sorting direction can be indicated per column.

Additions since Release 6.10

- `(dbtab_syntax)`
  In addition to flat character-type fields, strings and internal tables with a character-type line type can be specified. Specification of named data objects. Use in `DELETE` and `UPDATE`.

S

▶ (column_syntax)
In addition to internal tables with flat character-type line type, character-type fields and internal tables with a deep character-type line type can also be specified.

SELECT-OPTIONS

Syntax

```
SELECT-OPTIONS selcrit FOR {dobj|(name)}
               [OBLIGATORY|NO-DISPLAY]
               [VISIBLE LENGTH vlen]
               [NO-EXTENSION]
               [NO INTERVALS]
               [MODIF ID modid]
               [DEFAULT val1 [TO val2]
                        [OPTION opt] [SIGN sign]]
               [LOWER CASE]
               [MATCHCODE OBJECT search_help]
               [MEMORY ID pid]
               [HELP-REQUEST  [FOR {LOW|HIGH}]]
               [VALUE-REQUEST [FOR {LOW|HIGH}]]
               [NO DATABASE SELECTION].
```

Effect

Declares an internal selection table selcrit for a selection criterion and creates the corresponding input fields in the current selection screen.

Additions

▶ FOR {dobj|(name)}
Specifies the data type by statically referring to a data object dobj, or specifies the data type as c of length 45 and displays the input fields according to the type specified dynamically in name.

▶ OBLIGATORY
Defines the first input field as an obligatory field.

▶ NO-DISPLAY
No input fields are created in the selection screen.

▶ VISIBLE LENGTH vlen
Determines the visible length of the input fields to be vlen.

▶ NO-EXTENSION
Avoids multiple selection.

- `NO INTERVALS`
  Only the first input field is created in the selection screen.
- `MODIF ID modid`
  Assigns the input fields to the modification group `modid`.
- `DEFAULT val1 [TO val2] [OPTION opt] [SIGN sign]`
  Defines start values `val1`, `val2`, `opt` and `sign` for the first line of the selection table.
- `LOWER CASE`
  Avoids converting the content of character-type data objects into upper case letters during the transfer between input fields and internal table.
- `MATCHCODE OBJECT search_help`
  Links the input fields to a search help `search_help` from the ABAP dictionary.
- `MEMORY ID pid`
  Links the first input field to the SPA/GPA parameter `pid` in the SAP memory.
- `[HELP-REQUEST] [VALUE-REQUEST] [FOR {LOW|HIGH}]`
  Enables self-defined field and input helps for the first or second input field in logical databases.
- `NO DATABASE SELECTION`
  After the selection screen processing, the selection table is not transferred as a free selection to the logical database.

S

SELECTION-SCREEN

Syntax

```
SELECTION-SCREEN { { COMMENT [/][pos](len)
                     { text | {[text] FOR FIELD sel} }
                     [VISIBLE LENGTH vlen]
                     [MODIF ID modid] }
                 | { FUNCTION KEY n }
                 | { POSITION pos }
                 | { PUSHBUTTON [/][pos](len)
                     button_text USER-COMMAND fcode
                     [VISIBLE LENGTH vlen]
                     [MODIF ID modid] }
                 | { SKIP [n] }
                 | { ULINE [[/][pos](len)]
```

```
                          [MODIF ID modid] } }
                      [FOR {TABLE|NODE} node [ID id]].
```

Effect

Generates basic screen elements in the current selection screen.

Additions

- `COMMENT text | {[text] FOR FIELD sel}`
  Creates an output field containing the text `text`; the output field can be assigned to a parameter or selection criterion `sel`.
- `FUNCTION KEY n`
  Activates one of the predefined pushbuttons with the function codes "FC01" through "FC05" in the application toolbar.
- `POSITION pos`
  Positions the following screen element within a line.
- `PUSHBUTTON button_text USER-COMMAND fcode`
  Creates a pushbutton containing the text `button_text` and the function code `fcode`.
- `SKIP [n]`
  Creates one or `n` blank lines.
- `ULINE`
  Creates a horizontal line.
- `[/][pos](len)`
  Specifies the position of the screen element.
- `VISIBLE LENGTH vlen`
  Determines the visible length of the screen element to be `vlen`.
- `MODIF ID modid`
  Assigns the screen element to the modification group `modid`.
- `FOR {TABLE|NODE} node`
  Assigns the screen element in a logical database to a node `node` of the corresponding structure.
- `ID id`
  Defines an ID `id` consisting of no more than three characters for the screen element in a logical database.

Addition since Release 6.20

- `VISIBLE LENGTH vlen`
  In combination with `PUSHBUTTON`.

SELECTION-SCREEN—BEGIN OF

Syntax

```
SELECTION-SCREEN BEGIN OF SCREEN dynnr
  { {[TITLE title] [AS WINDOW]}
  | {AS SUBSCREEN [NO INTERVALS] [NESTING LEVEL n]} }.
...
SELECTION-SCREEN END OF SCREEN dynnr.
```

Effect

Defines a self-contained selection screen with dynpro number dynnr. The selection-screen elements are declared in between the two statements. Selection-screen elements that are declared outside these statements are part of the standard selection screen with dynpro number 1,000.

Additions

- TITLE title
  Specifies a title title of the title bar.
- AS WINDOW
  Definition of a selection screen for a modal dialog box.
- AS SUBSCREEN
  Definition of a selection screen as a subscreen dynpro.
- NO INTERVALS
  Sets the NO INTERVALS addition for all selection criteria of the selection screen.
- NESTING LEVEL n
  Adjusts the width of the subscreen within tabstrips.

S

SELECTION-SCREEN—BLOCK

Syntax

```
SELECTION-SCREEN BEGIN OF BLOCK block
                                [WITH FRAME [TITLE title]]
                                [NO INTERVALS].
...
SELECTION-SCREEN END OF BLOCK block.
```

Effect

Defines a block called block in the current selection screen.

Additions

- `WITH FRAME`
  Creates a frame around the block.
- `TITLE title`
  Creates a title `title` for the block.
- `NO INTERVALS`
  Sets the `NO INTERVALS` addition for all selection criteria of the block.

SELECTION-SCREEN—LINE

Syntax

```
SELECTION-SCREEN BEGIN OF LINE.
...
SELECTION-SCREEN END OF LINE.
```

Effect

Defines a line in the current selection screen in which screen elements can be positioned with `SELECTION-SCREEN POSITION`.

SELECTION-SCREEN—TABBED BLOCK

Syntax

```
SELECTION-SCREEN BEGIN OF TABBED BLOCK tblock FOR n LINES.
...
SELECTION-SCREEN END OF BLOCK tblock.
```

Effect

Defines a tabstrip or subscreen area called `tblock` in the current selection screen.

Addition

- `FOR n LINES`
  Defines the number of lines in the tabstrip area to be `n`.

SELECTION-SCREEN—VERSION

Syntax

```
SELECTION-SCREEN BEGIN OF VERSION vers text.
...
SELECTION-SCREEN END OF VERSION vers.
```

Effect

Defines a version `vers` of the standard selection screen in a logical database.

Addition

- `text`
  Specifies a help text for the version.

SELECTION-SCREEN DYNAMIC SELECTIONS

Syntax

```
SELECTION-SCREEN DYNAMIC SELECTIONS
                 FOR {NODE|TABLE} node [ID id].
```

Effect

Provides a node `node` of the structure of a logical database for free selections.

Addition

- `ID id`
  Defines an ID `id` consisting of no more than three characters for the node.

S

SELECTION-SCREEN EXCLUDE

Syntax

```
SELECTION-SCREEN EXCLUDE { {PARAMETERS parameter}
                         | {SELECT-OPTIONS selcrit}
                         | {RADIOBUTTON GROUPS radi}
                         | {BLOCKS block}
                         | {IDS id} }.
```

Effect

Removes the specified element from a version of the standard selection screen in a logical database.

Additions

- `PARAMETERS parameter`
  Removes a parameter `parameter`.
- `SELECT-OPTIONS selcrit`
  Removes a selection criterion `selcrit`.

- `RADIOBUTTON GROUPS radi`
  Removes a radio-button group `radi`.
- `BLOCKS block`
  Removes a block `block`.
- `IDS id`
  Removes all elements with the ID `id`.

SELECTION-SCREEN FIELD SELECTION

Syntax

```
SELECTION-SCREEN FIELD SELECTION
                 FOR {NODE|TABLE} node [ID id].
```

Effect

Provides a node `node` of the structure of a logical database for the field selection.

Addition

- `ID id`
  Defines an ID `id` consisting of no more than three characters for the node.

SELECTION-SCREEN INCLUDE

Syntax

```
SELECTION-SCREEN INCLUDE
  { { PARAMETERS parameter [OBLIGATORY [OFF]]
                           [MODIF ID modid] }
  | { SELECT-OPTIONS selcrit [OBLIGATORY [OFF]]
                             [NO INTERVALS [OFF]]
                             [NO-EXTENSIONS [OFF]]
                             [MODIF ID modid] }
  | { COMMENT [/][pos](len) text [FOR FIELD sel]
                                 [MODIF ID modid] }
  | { PUSHBUTTON [/][pos](len) button_text
                 [USER-COMMAND fcode]
                 [MODIF ID modid] }
  | { BLOCKS block } }
  [ID id].
```

Effect

Includes screen elements of another selection screen.

Additions

- `PARAMETERS parameter`
  Includes the screen elements of a parameter `parameter`.
- `SELECT-OPTIONS selcrit`
  Includes the screen elements of a selection criterion `selcrit`.
- `COMMENT [/][pos](len) text`
  Includes an output field at the position specified in `pos` and `len`.
- `PUSHBUTTON [/][pos](len) button_text [USER-COMMAND fcode]`
  Includes a pushbutton at the position specified in `pos` and `len`. The function code is either included or specified as `fcode`.
- `BLOCKS block`
  Includes a block `block` or a tabstrip area with all elements.
- `[OBLIGATORY [OFF]] [NO INTERVALS [OFF]] [NO-EXTENSIONS [OFF]] [MODIF ID modid] [FOR FIELD sel]`
  Overwrites the corresponding properties of the included element.
- `ID id`
  Defines an ID `id` consisting of no more than three characters for the included screen element in a logical database.

S

SELECTION-SCREEN TAB

Syntax

```
SELECTION-SCREEN TAB (len) tab USER-COMMAND fcode
                 [DEFAULT [PROGRAM prog] SCREEN dynnr].
```

Effect

Defines in a tabstrip area a tab title called `tab` that has the length `len` and the function code `fcode`.

Addition

- `DEFAULT [PROGRAM prog] SCREEN dynnr`
  Assigns a subscreen dynpro `dynnr` of the program `prog` to the tab title.

SET BIT

Syntax

```
SET BIT bitpos OF byte_string [TO val].
```

Effect

Sets the bit in the bit position `bitpos` of the data object `byte_string` to the value 1.

Addition

- `TO val`
  Sets the bit to the value `val`.

SET BLANK LINES

Syntax

```
SET BLANK LINES {ON|OFF}.
```

Effect

This statement defines whether the blank lines generated with `WRITE` are displayed.

SET COUNTRY

Syntax

```
SET COUNTRY cntry.
```

Effect

Determines the display of fractional portions and the date format for list outputs according to the country ID `cntry`.

SET CURSOR

Syntax

```
SET CURSOR { { FIELD field [LINE line]
                     [[DISPLAY|MEMORY] OFFSET off] }
           | { LINE line
                    [[DISPLAY|MEMORY] OFFSET off] }
           | { col lin } }.
```

Effect

Sets the cursor position in screens and lists.

Additions

- `FIELD field LINE line`
  Sets the cursor to the screen element or the field `field` which is displayed in a list; `line` specifies the line number of a table control, a step loop or a list.
- `LINE line`
  Positions the cursor to the table control, step loop, or list line specified in `line`.
- `OFFSET off`
  Determines the offset `off` the cursor is positioned to in the specified element.
- `col lin`
  Positions the cursor into the screen column and line specified in `col` and `lin`.

Addition since Release 6.20

- `DISPLAY|MEMORY`
  Differentiates between screen position and list buffer position in lists.

SET DATASET

Syntax

```
SET DATASET dest [POSITION {pos|{END OF FILE}}]
                 [ATTRIBUTES attr].
```

Release

6.10

Effect

Determines the properties of a file opened with `OPEN DATASET`.

Additions

- `POSITION {pos|{END OF FILE}}`
  Specifies the position of the file pointer as `pos` or as end of file (prior to Release 6.40, `END-OF-FILE`).
- `ATTRIBUTES attr`
  Specifies the properties of the file in the `attr` structure of the DSET_ATTRIBUTES type.

SET EXTENDED CHECK

Syntax

```
SET EXTENDED CHECK {ON|OFF}.
```

Effect

Switches the extended program check on or off.

SET HANDLER

Syntax

```
SET HANDLER handler1 handler2 ...
            [FOR oref|{ALL INSTANCES}]
            [ACTIVATION act].
```

Effect

Registers event handlers `handler1 handler2 ...` for class events.

Additions

- Specifies the handler methods `handler1 handler2 ...`:
  - `meth`—List of methods of the own class.
  - `oref->meth`—List of methods of referenced objects.
  - `class=>meth`—List of static methods of the classes specified.
- `FOR { oref | {ALL INSTANCES} }`
  Registers event-handler instances for an object referenced via `oref` or for all objects that can trigger the event.
- `ACTIVATION act`
  Specifies registration or deregistration in `act`.

SET HOLD DATA

Syntax

```
SET HOLD DATA {ON|OFF}.
```

Effect

Activates or deactivates the functionality of the standard menu items **Hold Data**, **Set Data** and **Delete Data** in the GUI status of the current dynpro.

SET LANGUAGE

Syntax

```
SET LANGUAGE lang.
```

Effect

Loads the list headings and text symbols of the text pool of the language specified in `lang`.

SET LEFT SCROLL-BOUNDARY

Syntax

```
SET LEFT SCROLL-BOUNDARY [COLUMN col].
```

Effect

Defines the left boundary of a horizontally movable list-page area.

Addition

- `COLUMN col`
  Excludes from scrolling all positions placed to the left of `col`. If nothing is specified, the current cursor position is used as a boundary.

S

SET LOCALE

Syntax

```
SET LOCALE LANGUAGE lang [COUNTRY cntry] [MODIFIER mod].
```

Effect

Defines the text environment.

Additions

- `LANGUAGE lang`
  Specifies the language in `lang`.
- `COUNTRY cntry`
  Specifies the country key in `cntry`.
- `MODIFIER mod`
  Specifies the ID of a specific locale in `mod`.

SET MARGIN

Syntax

```
SET MARGIN macol [marow].
```

Effect

Defines the left-hand margin of a print list according to the columns specified in `macol` and the top margin according to the rows specified in `marow`.

SET PARAMETER

Syntax

```
SET PARAMETER ID pid FIELD dobj.
```

Effect

Sets the SPA/GPA parameter specified in `pid` to the value of `dobj` in the SAP memory.

SET PF-STATUS

Syntax

```
SET PF-STATUS status [OF PROGRAM prog]
                     [EXCLUDING fcode]
                     [IMMEDIATELY].
```

Effect

Sets the GUI status.

Additions

- `OF PROGRAM prog`
  Specifies the program `prog` in which the GUI status is defined.
- `EXCLUDING fcode`
  Deactivates functions of the GUI status by specifying function codes in a character string or an internal table `fcode`.
- `IMMEDIATELY`
  Sets the GUI status for the list that is currently displayed after an interactive list event.

SET PROPERTY—OLE

Syntax

```
SET PROPERTY OF ole attr = dobj [NO FLUSH].
```

Effect

Assigns the content of the data object `dobj` to the attribute `attr` of an automation object `ole` created with `CREATE OBJECT ole`.

Addition

- `NO FLUSH`
  Defines that the attribute isn't passed on to the presentation layer until the function module FLUSH is called or the screen is changed.

SET RUN TIME ANALYZER

Syntax

```
SET RUN TIME ANALYZER {ON|OFF}.
```

Effect

Defines the units of a program which are to be measured with the runtime analysis tool.

SET RUN TIME CLOCK

Syntax

```
SET RUN TIME CLOCK RESOLUTION {HIGH|LOW}.
```

Effect

Defines the measurement accuracy for the `GET RUN TIME` statement.

SET SCREEN

Syntax

```
SET SCREEN dynnr.
```

Effect

Defines the dynpro with dynpro number `dynnr` as a follow-up dynpro to the current dynpro.

SET TITLEBAR

Syntax

```
SET TITLEBAR title [OF PROGRAM prog]
                   [WITH text1 ... text9].
```

Effect

Sets the GUI title.

Additions

- `OF PROGRAM prog`
  Specifies the program `prog` in which the GUI title is defined.
- `WITH text1 ... text9`
  Replaces the GUI title placeholders with the contents of the data objects `text1 ... text9`.

SET UPDATE TASK

Syntax

```
SET UPDATE TASK LOCAL.
```

Effect

Determines that—once the `COMMIT WORK` statement is run– high-priority update function modules registered with `CALL FUNCTION ... IN UPDATE TASK` are executed directly in the current work process and within the current database LUW.

SET USER-COMMAND

Syntax

```
SET USER-COMMAND fcode.
```

Effect

Triggers a list event by using a function code specified in `fcode`.

SHIFT

Syntax

```
SHIFT dobj [ { [ {BY num PLACES} | {UP TO sub_string} ]
               [LEFT|RIGHT] [CIRCULAR] }
```

```
            | { {LEFT DELETING LEADING}
              | {RIGHT DELETING TRAILING} pattern} ]
            [IN {BYTE|CHARACTER} MODE].
```

Effect
Moves bytes or characters within a byte or character string dobj.

Additions
- BY num PLACES
  Moves the string by num bytes or characters.
- UP TO sub_string
  Moves the string to the substring specified in sub_string.
- [LEFT|RIGHT] [CIRCULAR]
  Moves the string to the left or right, where CIRCULAR re-inserts characters that have been moved out on the other side.
- {LEFT DELETING LEADING}|{RIGHT DELETING TRAILING} pattern
  Moves the string to the left or right by one position until the content of the first or last position of dobj is contained in pattern.

Addition since Release 6.10
- IN {BYTE|CHARACTER} MODE
  Determines byte or character string processing.

SKIP

Syntax

```
SKIP { [n]
     | {TO LINE line} }.
```

Effect
Positions the list cursor in a line of the current list.

Additions
- n
  Positions the list cursor n lines below the current line. If nothing is specified, n is implicitly set to 1.
- TO LINE line
  Positions the list cursor in line line.

SORT

Syntax

```
SORT [ASCENDING|DESCENDING]
     [AS TEXT]
     [STABLE]
     [BY {field1 [ASCENDING|DESCENDING] [AS TEXT]}
         {field2 [ASCENDING|DESCENDING] [AS TEXT]}
         ...].
```

Effect

Sorts the extract data set of the program by the field group `header`.

Additions

- `ASCENDING`
  Sorts in ascending order.
- `DESCENDING`
  Sorts in descending order.
- `AS TEXT`
  Sorts text-type components according to the locale of the current text environment.
- `STABLE`
  Defines stable sorting that maintains the relative sort order of lines that are not involved.
- `BY field1 ... field2 ...`
  Sorts by the fields `field1 field2 ...` instead of the field group `header`.

SORT itab

Syntax

```
SORT itab [STABLE]
          { { [ASCENDING|DESCENDING]
              [AS TEXT]
              [BY {comp1 [ASCENDING|DESCENDING] [AS TEXT]}
                  {comp2 [ASCENDING|DESCENDING] [AS TEXT]}
                  ... ] }
          | { [BY (otab)] } }.
```

Effect

Sorts an internal table `itab` by the table key or a specified sort key.

Additions

- `STABLE`
  Defines stable sorting that maintains the relative sort order of lines which are not involved.
- `ASCENDING`
  Sorts in ascending order.
- `DESCENDING`
  Sorts in descending order.
- `AS TEXT`
  Sorts text-type components according to the locale of the current text environment.
- `BY comp1 ... comp2 ...`
  Sorts by the specified components `comp1 comp2 ...` instead of the table key.

Addition since Release 7.0

- `BY (otab)`
  Sorts by the sort order specified in table `otab` of the ABAP_SORT-ORDER_TAB type, instead of sorting by the table key.

S

SPLIT

Syntax

```
SPLIT dobj AT sep INTO
      { {result1 result2 ...} | {TABLE result_tab} }
      [IN {BYTE|CHARACTER} MODE].
```

Effect

Splits up a byte or character string `dobj`.

Additions

- `AT sep`
  Specifies the separator string `sep` according to which the string is split.
- `INTO { {result1 result2 ...} | {TABLE result_tab} }`
  Specifies the target fields either as a list `result1 result2 ...` or as lines of the internal table `result_tab`.

Addition since Release 6.10

- `IN {BYTE|CHARACTER} MODE`
  Determines byte- or character-string processing.

sql_cond

Syntax

```
{ {col1 {=|EQ|<>|NE|>|GT|<|LT|>=|GE|<=|LE}
          { {dobj}
          | {col2}
          | {[ALL|ANY|SOME] subquery} }}
| {col [NOT] BETWEEN dobj1 AND dobj2}
| {col [NOT] LIKE dobj [ESCAPE esc]}
| {col [NOT] IN (dobj1, dobj2 ...)}
| {col [NOT] IN seltab}
| {col IS [NOT] NULL}
| {(cond_syntax)}
| {[NOT] EXISTS subquery}
| {col [NOT] IN subquery} }
```

Effect

Condition for contents of columns `col` after the `WHERE` addition in Open SQL statements. Conditions can be explicitly parenthesized with `( )`, linked with `AND` and `OR`, and negated with `NOT`.

Additions

- `=|EQ|<>|NE|>|GT|<|LT|>=|GE|<=|LE`
  Relational operators: Column contents can be compared with data objects `dobj`, contents of other columns `col2`, and the result of a subquery *`subquery`* (see `subquery` entry).
- `ALL|ANY|SOME`
  Must be specified if the result of the subquery *`subquery`* (see `subquery` entry) consists of multiple rows.
- `BETWEEN`
  Checks whether the column content is within an interval.
- `LIKE dobj [ESCAPE esc]`
  Checks whether the column content matches a pattern in `dobj`. With `ESCAPE` an escape character `esc` can be defined for the wildcard characters "%" and "_".
- `IN (dobj1, dobj2 ...)`
  Checks whether the column content is part of a value list `dobj1`, `dobj2`, ...
- `IN seltab`
  Checks whether the column content meets the conditions of a selection table `seltab`.

- IS NULL
  Checks whether the column content is the zero value.
- (cond_syntax)
  Dynamic specification of the condition in cond_syntax.
- EXISTS *subquery*
  Checks the resulting set of the subquery *subquery* (see subquery entry).
- col IN *subquery*
  Checks if the column content is contained in the resulting set of the subquery *subquery* (see subquery entry).
- NOT
  Negates a condition.

Addition since Release 6.10

- (cond_syntax)
  In addition to internal tables with flat character-type line type, character-type fields and internal tables with a deep character-type line type can also be specified.

S

START-OF-SELECTION

Syntax

```
START-OF-SELECTION.
```

Effect

Initiates an event block whose event is triggered in executable programs after the standard selection-screen processing.

STATICS

Syntax

```
STATICS dobj[(len)] [TYPE { {abap_type [LENGTH len]
                                       [DECIMALS dec]}
                          | {[LINE OF] type}
                          | {REF TO type}
                          | { {{[STANDARD] TABLE}
                              |{SORTED TABLE}
                              |{HASHED TABLE}}
                             OF [REF TO] type
                             [WITH [UNIQUE|NON-UNIQUE]
```

```
                    {KEY comp1 comp2 ...}
                   |{DEFAULT KEY}]
             [INITIAL SIZE n]
             [WITH HEADER LINE]}
           | {RANGE OF type
                [INITIAL SIZE n]
                [WITH HEADER LINE]} }]
| [LIKE { {[LINE OF] dobj}
        | {REF TO dobj}
        | { {{[STANDARD] TABLE}
              |{SORTED TABLE}
              |{HASHED TABLE}}
             OF [REF TO] dobj
             [WITH [UNIQUE|NON-UNIQUE]
                    {KEY comp1 comp2 ...}
                   |{DEFAULT KEY}]
             [INITIAL SIZE n]
             [WITH HEADER LINE]}
           | {RANGE OF dobj
                [INITIAL SIZE n]
                [WITH HEADER LINE]} }]
  [VALUE { val | {IS INITIAL} }].
```

Effect

Declares a static local data object `dobj` in a subroutine, a function module, or a static method.

Additions

- `(len)`
  Determines the length when referring to generic built-in ABAP types.
- `TYPE`
  Determines the type by referring to a data type.
- `LIKE`
  Determines the type by referring to a data object.
- `DECIMALS dec`
  Determines the number of fractional portions when referring to generic built-in ABAP type `p`.
- `LINE OF`
  Determines the type by referring to the line type of an internal table.

▶ REF TO
Creates a reference variable.

▶ {[STANDARD] TABLE}|{SORTED TABLE}|{HASHED TABLE}
Creates a standard, sorted or hashed table.

▶ WITH {[UNIQUE|NON-UNIQUE] {KEY comp1 comp2 ...}}|{DEFAULT KEY}
Defines a unique or non-unique table key. The components of the key are either specified explicitly or defined by a standard key.

▶ INITIAL SIZE n
Defines the initial memory allocation for an internal table.

▶ RANGE OF
Defines a ranges table with the line type of a selection table.

▶ VALUE { val | {IS INITIAL} }
Sets the start value of the data object to val or to the initial value.

Addition since Release 6.10

▶ LENGTH len
Determines the length when referring to generic built-in ABAP types.

Obsolete addition

▶ WITH HEADER LINE
Defines a header line having the same name as dobj for an internal table.

S

STOP

Syntax

```
STOP.
```

Effect

Leaves the AT SELECTION-SCREEN, START-OF-SELECTION and GET event blocks and triggers the END-OF-SELECTION event.

SUBMIT

Syntax

```
SUBMIT {rep|(name)}
  [USING SELECTION-SCREEN dynnr]
  [VIA SELECTION-SCREEN]
  [USING SELECTION-SET variant]
```

```
  [USING SELECTION-SETS OF PROGRAM prog]
  [WITH SELECTION-TABLE rspar]
{ [WITH sel1 { {{EQ|NE|CP|NP|GE|LT|LE|GT} dobj [SIGN sign]}
             | {[NOT] BETWEEN dobj1 AND dobj2 [SIGN sign]}
             | {IN rtab} }]
  [WITH sel2 { {{EQ|NE|CP|NP|GE|LT|LE|GT} dobj [SIGN sign]}
             | {[NOT] BETWEEN dobj1 AND dobj2 [SIGN sign]}
             | {IN rtab} }]
   ... }
  [WITH FREE SELECTIONS texpr]
  [LINE-SIZE width]
  [LINE-COUNT page_lines]
  { [EXPORTING LIST TO MEMORY]
  | [TO SAP-SPOOL SPOOL PARAMETERS pri_params
                [ARCHIVE PARAMETERS arc_params]
                WITHOUT SPOOL DYNPRO] }
  [[USER user] VIA JOB job NUMBER n]
  [AND RETURN].
```

Effect

Calls an executable program.

Additions

- `{rep|(name)}`
  Specifies the program statically as `rep` or dynamically in `name`.
- `USING SELECTION-SCREEN dynnr`
  Specifies the selection screen `dynnr` to be called. If nothing is specified, the standard selection screen is called.
- `VIA SELECTION-SCREEN`
  Displays the selection screen called. If nothing is specified, selection-screen processing takes place in the background.
- `USING SELECTION-SET variant`
  Provides the values of a variant `variant` to the selection screen.
- `USING SELECTION-SETS OF PROGRAM prog`
  Specifies a program `prog` whose variants are being used.
- `WITH SELECTION-TABLE rspar`
  Provides values from an internal table `rspar` of the RSPARAMS line type to the selection screen.
- `WITH sel1 ... WITH sel2 ...`
  Provides individual parameters or selection criteria `sel1 sel2 ...` of the selection screen with values:

- {EQ|NE|CP|NP|GE|LT|LE|GT} dobj [SIGN sign]—Transfer of a single value dobj with relational operators and a specification for the SIGN column of the selection table.
- [NOT] BETWEEN dobj1 AND dobj2 [SIGN sign]—Transfer of an interval dobj1 to dobj2 with optional operator NOT and and a specification for the SIGN column of the selection table.
- IN rtab—Transfer of a ranges table rtab.

- WITH FREE SELECTIONS texpr
  Provides values from an internal table texpr of the RSDS_TEXPR type from type pool RSDS for the free selection of a logical database's selection screen.
- LINE-SIZE width
  Sets the line width of the called program's basic list to width characters.
- LINE-COUNT page_lines
  Sets the page length of the called program's basic list to page_lines lines.
- EXPORTING LIST TO MEMORY
  Stores the basic list of the called program as an internal table of the ABAPLIST type in the ABAP memory. Can only be used in combination with AND RETURN.
- TO SAP-SPOOL
  Creates a spool request for the basic list of the called program, with the following parameters:
  - SPOOL PARAMETERS pri_params—Print parameters in a structure pri_params of the PRI_PARAMS type.
  - ARCHIVE PARAMETERS arc_params—Archiving parameters in a structure arc_params of the ARC_PARAMS type.
  - WITHOUT SPOOL DYNPRO—Suppresses the print dialog box.
- [USER user] VIA JOB job NUMBER n
  Schedules the execution of the called program as a background task with number n in background job job. Can only be used in combination with AND RETURN. With user a user name can be specified for the background task.
- AND RETURN
  On completion of the program call the program execution of the calling program continues after the SUBMIT statement. Otherwise the calling program will terminate.

subquery

Syntax

```
( SELECT [DISTINCT]
         { *
         | { {col1|aggregate( [DISTINCT] col1 )} [AS a1]
             {col2|aggregate( [DISTINCT] col2 )} [AS a2]
             ... }
         | (column_syntax) }
         FROM { { {dbtab [AS tabalias]}
                | { [(] {dbtab_left [AS tabalias_left]} | join
                        {[INNER] JOIN}|{LEFT [OUTER] JOIN}
                        {dbtab_right [AS tabalias_right]
                                    ON sql_cond} [)]}
                | (dbtab_syntax) [AS tabalias] }
                [UP TO n ROWS]
                [CLIENT SPECIFIED]
                [BYPASSING BUFFER] }
         [WHERE sql_cond]
         [GROUP BY {col1 col2 ... }|(column_syntax)]
         [HAVING sql_cond] )
```

Effect

SELECT statement in parenthesis that can be used in conditions *sql_cond* (see sql_cond entry) of Open SQL statements for a subquery.

Additions

- DISTINCT
  Excludes duplicate rows from the resulting set.
- *
  Reads all columns.
- col1 ... col2 ...
  Reads individual columns col1 col2 ...
- *aggregate*([DISTINCT] col1) *aggregate*([DISTINCT] col2) ...
  Evaluates aggregate functions *aggregate* (see aggregate entry) for columns col1 col2 ...; duplicate arguments can be excluded.
- AS a1 ... AS a2 ...
  Defines alternative column names a1 a2 ...
- (column_syntax)
  Specifies the columns as content of column_syntax.

- FROM dbtab [AS tabalias]
  Specifies a database table dbtab.
- FROM [(] {dbtab_left [AS tabalias_left]} | join
  {[INNER] JOIN}|{LEFT [OUTER] JOIN}
  {dbtab_right [AS tabalias_right] ON *sql_cond*} [)]
  Combines a database table dbtab_left, or a join expression join with a database table dbtab_right, to a join expression. Inner and outer joins can be built with join conditions *sql_cond* that are—with a few restrictions—identical to the WHERE conditions.
- (dbtab_syntax)
  Specifies the database tables as content of source_syntax.
- AS tabalias
  Defines an alternative table name tabalias.
- UP TO n ROWS
  Limits the number of rows read to n.
- CLIENT SPECIFIED
  Switches off the automatic client handling.
- BYPASSING BUFFER
  Bypasses the SAP buffering.
- WHERE *sql_cond*
  Restricts the resulting set by a condition *sql_cond* (see sql_cond entry). The condition can consist of various logical expressions.
- GROUP BY { col1 col2 ... | (column_syntax) }
  Condenses groups of rows with the same content in the columns col1 col2 ... into a single row of the resulting set; the columns can be specified dynamically in column_syntax.
- HAVING *sql_cond*
  Restricts the rows that were condensed into groups in the resulting set by a condition *sql_cond* (see sql_cond entry).

Additions since Release 6.10

- (dbtab_syntax)
  In addition to flat character-type fields, strings and internal tables with a character-type line type can be specified. Specification of named data objects. Use in DELETE and UPDATE.
- (column_syntax)
  In addition to internal tables with flat character-type line type, character-type fields and internal tables with a deep character-type line type can be specified.

S

SUBTRACT

Syntax

```
SUBTRACT dobj1 FROM dobj2.
```

Effect

Subtracts the content of a numerical data object dobj1 from the content of a numerical data object dobj2 and assigns the result to dobj2.

SUBTRACT-CORRESPONDING

Syntax

```
SUBTRACT-CORRESPONDING struc1 FROM struc2.
```

Release

Obsolete

Effect

Subtracts the components of a structure struc1 from components having the same name of a structure struc2.

SUM

Syntax

```
SUM.
```

Effect

Sums up the numerical components of a control level during the control-level processing of an internal table.

SUMMARY

Syntax

```
SUMMARY.
```

Release

Obsolete

Effect

Specifies the intensity of the background color of a list.

SUMMING

Syntax

```
SUMMING dobj.
```

Release

Obsolete

Effect

After the SUMMING statement the value of dobj is added to the content of SUM_dobj with each WRITE statement.

SUPPLY

Syntax

```
SUPPLY key1 = f1 key2 = f2 ... TO CONTEXT context_ref.
```

Release

Obsolete

S

Effect

Provides the values of data objects f1 f2 ... to the key fields key1 key2 ... of a context instance referenced by context_ref.

SUPPRESS DIALOG

Syntax

```
SUPPRESS DIALOG.
```

Effect

When specified at PBO, the current dynpro is processed without any screen display.

SYNTAX-CHECK

Syntax

```
SYNTAX-CHECK FOR itab MESSAGE mess LINE lin WORD wrd
                 [PROGRAM prog] [DIRECTORY ENTRY dir]
                 [WITH CURRENT SWITCHSTATES]
                 [INCLUDE incl]
```

```
                 [OFFSET off]
                 [MESSAGE-ID mid].
```

Effect

Checks the syntax of the source code in `itab` and returns the first error message, the first line that contains an error, and the first incorrect word in `mess`, `lin` and `wrd`.

Additions

- `PROGRAM prog`
  Defines the program properties by referring to a program `prog`.
- `DIRECTORY ENTRY dir`
  Determines the program properties by specifying a structure of the TRDIR type in `dir`.
- `INCLUDE incl`
  Returns the name of the include program in which the error occurs in `incl`.
- `OFFSET off`
  Returns the offset of the error in the line in `off`.
- `MESSAGE-ID mid`
  Returns the key of the error message from the TRMSG table in `mid`.

Addition since Release 7.0

- `WITH CURRENT SWITCHSTATES`
  Determines which switch configuration is used for the syntax check.

TABLES

Syntax

```
TABLES table_wa.
```

Effect

Declares an interface work area `table_wa` for the data transfer from and to dynpros and from logical databases.

TABLES *

Syntax

```
TABLES *table_wa.
```

Release

Obsolete

Effect

Declares an additional interface work area `*table_wa`.

TOP-OF-PAGE

Syntax

```
TOP-OF-PAGE [DURING LINE-SELECTION].
```

Effect

Initiates an event block whose event is triggered during the creation of a basic list when a new page is created.

Addition

- `DURING LINE-SELECTION`
  Initiates an event block whose event is triggered during the creation of a details list when a new page is created.

T

TRANSFER

Syntax

```
TRANSFER dobj TO dset [LENGTH len]
                      [NO END OF LINE].
```

Effect

Transfers the data of the data object `dobj` into the file specified in `dset`.

Addition

- `LENGTH len`
  Limits the number of characters or bytes to be transferred to `len`.

Addition since Release 6.40

- `NO END OF LINE`
  Prevents the adding of end-of-line marks in text files or legacy text files.

TRANSLATE

Syntax

```
TRANSLATE dobj { {TO {UPPER|LOWER} CASE }
               | {USING pattern }
               | {[FROM CODE PAGE cp1]
                  [TO CODE PAGE cp2]}
               | {[FROM NUMBER FORMAT nf1]
                  [TO NUMBER FORMAT nf2]} }.
```

Effect

Translates the content of a data object `dobj`.

Additions

- `TO {UPPER|LOWER} CASE`
  Translates all lower case letters into upper case letters or vice versa.
- `USING pattern`
  Translates characters according to the rule specified by character pairs in the data object `pattern`.

Obsolete Additions

- `FROM|TO CODE PAGE`
  Translates the content from one code page into another code page.
- `FROM|TO NUMBER FORMAT`
  Translates the content from one number format into another number format.

TRUNCATE DATASET

Syntax

```
TRUNCATE DATASET dset AT {CURRENT POSITION}|{POSITION pos}.
```

Release

6.40

Effect

Sets the end of the file specified in `dset` to the position specified after `AT`.

Additions

- CURRENT POSITION
  Sets the end of the file to the current file pointer.
- POSITION pos
  Sets the end of the file to the position specified in pos.

TRY

Syntax

```
TRY.
    [try_block]
  [CATCH cx_class1 cx_class2 ... [INTO oref].
    [catch_block]]
    ...
  [CLEANUP [INTO oref].
    [cleanup_block]]
ENDTRY.
```

Release

6.10

Effect

Defines a monitored area try_block whose class-based exceptions cx_class1 cx_class2 ... can be handled in CATCH blocks catch_block. The CLEANUP block cleanup_block is executed if a class-based exception is triggered in the TRY block and not handled in a CATCH block of its own, but in that of an external TRY control structure.

Addition

- INTC oref
  Assigns a reference to the exception object to oref.

Addition since Release 6.20

- INTC oref
  Also possible after CLEANUP.

TYPE-POOL

Syntax

```
TYPE-POOL tpool.
```

Effect
Initiates a type pool tpool.

TYPE-POOLS

Syntax

```
TYPE-POOLS tpool.
```

Effect
This statement integrates type pool tpool in the current context.

TYPES

Syntax

```
TYPES dtype[(len)] {TYPE { {abap_type [LENGTH len]
                                      [DECIMALS dec]}
                         | {[LINE OF] type}
                         | {REF TO type}
                         | { {{[STANDARD] TABLE}
                             |{SORTED TABLE}
                             |{HASHED TABLE}}
                             OF [REF TO] type
                             [WITH [UNIQUE|NON-UNIQUE]
                                   {KEY comp1 comp2 ...}
                                   |{DEFAULT KEY}]
                             [INITIAL SIZE n]}
                           | {RANGE OF type
                                [INITIAL SIZE n]} }}
                 | {LIKE { {[LINE OF] dobj}
                         | {REF TO dobj}
                         | { {{[STANDARD] TABLE}
                             |{SORTED TABLE}
                             |{HASHED TABLE}
                             |{ANY TABLE}
                             |{INDEX TABLE}}
                             OF [REF TO] dobj
                             [WITH [UNIQUE|NON-UNIQUE]
                                   {KEY comp1 comp2 ...}
                                  |{DEFAULT KEY}]
                             [INITIAL SIZE n]}
```

```
                       | {RANGE OF dobj
                          [INITIAL SIZE n]} }}.
```

Effect

Defines a data type dtype.

Additions

- (len)
  Determines the length when referring to generic built-in ABAP types.
- TYPE
  Determines the type by referring to a data type.
- LIKE
  Determines the type by referring to a data object.
- DECIMALS dec
  Determines the number of fractional portions when referring to generic built-in ABAP type p.
- LINE OF
  Refers to the line type of an internal table.
- REF TO
  Creates a reference type.
- {[STANDARD] TABLE}|{SORTED TABLE}|{HASHED TABLE}|{ANY TABLE}|{INDEX TABLE}
  Creates a table type for the non-generic table types standard, sorted or hashed table. Also creates a table type for the generic table types ANY TABLE or INDEX TABLE.
- WITH {[UNIQUE|NON-UNIQUE] {KEY comp1 comp2 ...}}|{DEFAULT KEY}
  Defines a unique or non-unique table key. The components of the key are either specified explicitly or defined by a standard key.
- INITIAL SIZE n
  Defines the initial memory allocation for an internal table.
- RANGE OF
  Defines a ranges table with the line type of a selection table.

Addition since Release 6.10

- LENGTH len
  Determines the length when referring to generic built-in ABAP types.

T

TYPES BEGIN OF

Syntax

```
TYPES BEGIN OF struc_type.
  ...
  TYPES | INCLUDE ...
  ...
DATA END OF struc_type.
```

Effect

Defines a structured data type `struc_type` the components of which can be defined by any `TYPES` statement or included from other structures with `INCLUDE`.

TYPES—OCCURS

Syntax

```
TYPES dtype { {TYPE [REF TO] type}
            | {LIKE [REF TO] dobj} } OCCURS n.
```

Release

Obsolete

Effect

Declares a standard table type with a standard key and the initial memory allocation `n`.

Additions

- `TYPE`
  Determines the line type by referring to a data type.
- `LIKE`
  Determines the line type by referring to a data object.
- `REF TO`
  Creates the line type as reference type.

typing

Syntax

```
... { TYPE generic_type }
  | { TYPE {[LINE OF] complete_type}
         | {REF TO {data|complete_type|class|intf}} }
```

```
| { LIKE {[LINE OF] dobj}
      | {REF TO dobj} } ...
```

Effect

Typing of field symbols or formal parameters.

Additions

- `TYPE`
  Types by referring to a data type.
- `LIKE`
  Types by referring to a data object.
- `LINE OF`
  Types by referring to the line type of an internal table.
- `REF TO`
  Types as a reference type.

ULINE

Syntax

```
ULINE {[AT] [/][pos][(len)]} [NO-GAP].
```

Effect

Creates a continuous horizontal line in a list.

Additions

- `[AT] [/][pos][(len)]`
  Specifies the line feed /, the horizontal position `pos` and the length `len` of the line. If nothing is specified, a continuous line is created in a new line.
- `NO-GAP`
  Positions the list cursor directly after the output and not in the next but one position in the list buffer.

UNPACK

Syntax

```
UNPACK source TO destination.
```

U

Effect

Assigns the digits of a packed number `source` to the character-type variable `destination`.

UPDATE

Syntax

```
UPDATE {dbtab|(dbtab_syntax)} [CLIENT SPECIFIED]
       { { SET [col1 = f1 col2 = f2 ... ]
               [col1 = col1 + f1 col2 = col2 + f2 ...]
               [col1 = col1 - f1 col2 = col2 - f2 ...]
               [(expr_syntax1) (expr_syntax2) ...]
               [WHERE sql_cond] }
       | { FROM wa|{TABLE itab} } }.
```

Effect

Modifies rows in a database table.

Additions

- `{dbtab|(dbtab_syntax)}`
  Specifies the database table statically or dynamically.
- `CLIENT SPECIFIED`
  Switches off the automatic client handling.
- `SET col1 = f1 col2 = f2 ...`
  Assigns the contents of `f1 f2 ...` to the columns `col1 col2 ...`
- `SET col1 = col1 + f1 col2 = col2 + f2 ...`
  Adds the contents of `f1 f2 ...` to columns `col1 col2 ...`
- `SET col1 = col1 - f1 col2 = col2 - f2 ...`
  Subtracts the contents of `f1 f2 ...` from columns `col1 col2 ...`
- `WHERE` *`sql_cond`*
  Specifies the rows to be modified by a condition *`sql_cond`* (see `sql_cond` entry).
- `{FROM wa}|{FROM TABLE itab}`
  Overwrites rows with a work area `wa` or with the lines of an internal table `itab`.

Additions since Release 6.10

- `(dbtab_syntax)`
  In addition to flat character-type fields, strings and internal tables with a character-type line type can also be specified.

▶ SET (expr_syntax)
Dynamic specification of a modification in expr_syntax.

WAIT

Syntax

```
WAIT {UP TO t SECONDS}
   | {UNTIL log_exp [UP TO t SECONDS]}.
```

Effect

Interrupts the program execution.

Additions

▶ UP TO t SECONDS
Interrupts the program execution for (not more than) t seconds.

▶ UNTIL *log_exp*
Interrupts the program execution until the logical expression *log_exp* (see log_exp entry) after the callback routine of an asynchronous RFC is true.

WHILE

W

Syntax

```
WHILE log_exp
      [VARY dobj FROM dobj1 NEXT dobj2 [RANGE range]].
  [statement_block]
ENDWHILE.
```

Effect

Repeatedly executes the statement block statement_block in a loop as long as the logical expression *log_exp* (see log_exp entry) is true.

Addition since Release 6.10

▶ RANGE range
The data object range restricts the memory area that can be addressed with VARY.

Obsolete Addition

▶ VARY dobj FROM dobj1 NEXT dobj2
Assigns a value of the memory sequence defined by dobj1 and dobj2 to a variable dobj during each loop pass.

WINDOW

Syntax

```
WINDOW STARTING AT col1 lin1
       [ENDING  AT col2 lin2].
```

Effect

Defines the display of the current details list in a dialog box.

Additions

- `STARTING AT col1 lin1`
  Specifies the upper left-hand corner.
- `ENDING AT col2 lin2`
  Specifies the lower right-hand corner.

WRITE

Syntax

```
WRITE {[AT] [/][pos][(len|*|**)]} dobj
  [LEFT-JUSTIFIED|CENTERED|RIGHT-JUSTIFIED]
  [NO-GAP]
  [UNDER other_dobj]
  { { [EXPONENT exp]
      [NO-GROUPING]
      [NO-SIGN]
      [NO-ZERO]
      [CURRENCY cur]
      { { [DECIMALS dec]
          [ROUND scale] }
        | [UNIT unit] } }
    | [TIME ZONE tz] }
  [USING {{NO EDIT MASK}|{EDIT MASK mask}}]
  [DD/MM/YY|MM/DD/YY|DD/MM/YYYY|MM/DD/YYYY
  |DDMMYY|MMDDYY|YYMMDD]
  [COLOR { { { { COL_BACKGROUND
             | {1 | COL_HEADING }
             | {2 | COL_NORMAL }
             | {3 | COL_TOTAL }
             | {4 | COL_KEY }
             | {5 | COL_POSITIVE }
             | {6 | COL_NEGATIVE }
             | {7 | COL_GROUP } } [ON] }
```

```
              | OFF}
       | {= col} }]
 [INTENSIFIED [ {ON|OFF} | {= flag} ]]
 [INVERSE     [ {ON|OFF} | {= flag} ]]
 [HOTSPOT     [ {ON|OFF} | {= flag} ]]
 [INPUT       [ {ON|OFF} | {= flag} ]]
 [FRAMES      [ {ON|OFF} | {= flag} ]]
 [RESET]
 { [AS CHECKBOX]
 | [AS ICON]
 | [AS SYMBOL]
 | [AS LINE] }
 [QUICKINFO info].
```

Effect

Writes the content of the data object `dobj` into the current list.

Additions

- `[AT] [/][pos][(len)]`
  Specifies the line feed /, the horizontal position `pos` and the length `len` of the output.

- `LEFT-JUSTIFIED|CENTERED|RIGHT-JUSTIFIED`
  Specifies if the output is left-aligned, centered or right-aligned within the current output length.

- `NO-GAP`
  Positions the list cursor directly after the output and not in the next but one position in the list buffer.

- `UNDER other_dobj`
  The output is displayed in the current line, at the position at which the data object `other_dobj` was output in a previous `WRITE` statement.

- `EXPONENT exp`
  Defines the exponent for the output of data objects of data type `f`.

- `NO-GROUPING`
  When data objects of data type `i` or `p` are output, this addition suppresses the thousands separator.

- `NO-SIGN`
  When data objects of data type `i`, `p` or `f` are output, this addition suppresses the plus/minus sign.

W

- `NO-ZERO`
  Replaces zero signs with blanks.
- `CURRENCY cur`
  When data objects of data type `i` or `p` are output, this addition defines currency-dependent fractional portions by using a currency key `cur` from database table TCURX.
- `DECIMALS dec`
  When data objects of data types `i`, `p` or `f` are output, this addition defines the number of displayed fractional portions to be displayed to be `dec`.
- `ROUND scale`
  Multiplies the value of a data object of data type `p` by `10**(-scale)` before the output.
- `UNIT unit`
  When data objects of data type `p` are output, this addition truncates the fractional portions that have the value 0 and that lie beyond the accuracy level of a measurement unit `unit` from database table T006.
- `TIME ZONE tz`
  Formats a time stamp in connection with a time zone `tz`.
- `USING {{NO EDIT MASK}|{EDIT MASK mask}}`
  - `NO EDIT MASK`—Switches off the execution of an assigned conversion routine.
  - `EDIT MASK`—Either calls another conversion routine `mask` or defines a formatting template `mask`.
- `DD/MM/YY|MM/DD/YY|DD/MM/YYYY|MM/DD/YYYY|DDMMYY|MMDDYY|YYMMDD`
  Acts as a formatting template for the output of data objects of data type `d`.
- `COLOR`
  Sets the color as in the `FORMAT` statement, but refers to the current output.
- `INTENSIFIED`
  Sets the background color intensity as in the `FORMAT` statement, but refers to the current output.
- `INVERSE`
  Toggles between foreground and background colors in the current output.

- HOTSPOT
  Generates the current output as a hotspot to respond to single mouse clicks.
- INPUT
  Generates the current output as an input area.
- RESET
  Sets all settings except FRAMES to the OFF status for the current output.
- AS CHECKBOX
  Creates a single-character ready-for-input checkbox.
- AS ICON
  Creates an icon if the corresponding internal display is contained in dobj.
- AS SYMBOL
  Creates a symbol if the corresponding internal display is contained in dobj.
- AS LINE
  Creates a line element if the corresponding internal display is contained in dobj.
- QUICKINFO info
  Assigns a quick info text to an output.

W

Addition since Release 6.10

- FRAMES
  Controls the conversion of "-" and "|" into line elements in the current output.

Addition since Release 6.20

- (*|**)
  Determines the output length to the minimum or maximum length required in order to display all characters of dobj in Unicode systems. The length depends on the data type.

WRITE TO

Syntax

```
WRITE {source|(source_name)} TO destination
  [LEFT-JUSTIFIED|CENTERED|RIGHT-JUSTIFIED]
  {    [EXPONENT exp]
       [NO-GROUPING]
```

```
      [NO-SIGN]
      [NO-ZERO]
      [CURRENCY cur]
      { { [DECIMALS dec]
          [ROUND scale] }
        | [UNIT unit] } }
    | [TIME ZONE tz] }
  [USING {{NO EDIT MASK}|{EDIT MASK mask}}]
  [DD/MM/YY|MM/DD/YY|DD/MM/YYYY|MM/DD/YYYY
  |DDMMYY|MMDDYY|YYMMDD].
```

Effect

Writes the content of a data object specified statically dynamically in source_name into the variable destinatio

Additions

- Similar to the WRITE statement for lists (see previous entry) but referring to the target field destination.

WRITE TO itab

Syntax

```
WRITE dobj TO itab[+off][(len)] INDEX idx
      [format_options].
```

Release

Obsolete

Effect

Writes the content of a data object into the line of an internal table itab that has the index idx.

Additions

- [+off][(len)]
  Writes into the section of the table line which begins at position pos and has the length len.
- format_options
  Additions similar to the WRITE TO statement for variables (see previous entry).

Tables with ABAP Information

Table 1: Elementary ABAP Types

The following table lists the built-in elementary ABAP types.

Name	Meaning
`c`	Text field
`d`	Date field
`f`	Floating point number
`i`	Integer
`n`	Numeric text field
`p`	Packed number
`string`	Text string
`t`	Time field
`x`	Byte field
`xstring`	Byte string

Table 2: Generic ABAP Types

The following table lists the built-in generic ABAP types.

Name	Meaning
`any`	Any data type
`any table`	Any internal table
`clike`	Character-type (since Release 6.10)
`csequence`	Text-type (since Release 6.10)
`data`	Any data type
`hashed table`	Hashed table
`index table`	Index table
`numeric`	Numeric (since Release 6.10)
`object`	Any object type
`simple`	Elementary data type (since Release 6.10)
`sorted table`	Sorted table
`standard table`	Standard table
`table`	Standard table
`xsequence`	Byte-type (since Release 6.10)

Table 3: Built-In Data Objects

The following table lists the implicitly existing data objects (except for system fields, see also next table).

Name	Meaning
`me`	Self-reference in instance methods
`screen`	Structure of dynpro element properties
`space`	Blank character

Table 4: System Fields

The following table lists the implicitly existing system fields that provide information on the current system statuses.

Name	Meaning
`sy-abcde`	Contains the Latin alphabet.
`sy-batch`	Indicates background processing.
`sy-binpt`	Indicates processing of batch input sessions.
`sy-calld`	Indicates program calls.
`sy-callr`	Indicates where list printout was started.
`sy-colno`	Current position during list creation.
`sy-cpage`	Page number of uppermost page displayed during a list event.
`sy-cprog`	Name of a calling program
`sy-cucol`	Horizontal cursor position in the current screen
`sy-curow`	Vertical cursor position in the current screen
`sy-datar`	Indicates input in the current screen.
`sy-datlo`	Local date of the current user
`sy-datum`	Local date of the SAP system
`sy-dayst`	Indicates daylight saving time.
`sy-dbcnt`	Number of table rows edited in Open SQL
`sy-dbnam`	Linked logical database
`sy-dbsys`	Central database system
`sy-dyngr`	Screen group of the current dynpro
`sy-dynnr`	Number of the current dynpro
`sy-fdayw`	Factory calendar weekday
`sy-fdpos`	Found position in search operations
`sy-host`	Name of the current application server
`sy-index`	Loop index

sy-langu	Language of the current locale
sy-ldbpg	Database program of the linked logical database
sy-lilli	List line at list event
sy-linct	Page length of the current list
sy-linno	Current list line
sy-linsz	Line width of the current list
sy-lisel	Content of list line at list event
sy-listi	List level at list event
sy-lcopc	Number of lines in current table control
sy-lsind	Current list level
sy-macol	Left margin for list printout
sy-mandt	Current client ID
sy-marow	Top margin for list printout
sy-modno	Current external mode
sy-msgid	Message class of a message
sy-msgno	Message number of a message
sy-msgty	Message type of a message
sy-msgv1	Content of 1st placeholder of a message
sy-msgv2	Content of 2nd placeholder of a message
sy-msgv3	Content of 3rd placeholder of a message
sy-msgv4	Content of 4th placeholder of a message
sy-opsys	OS of the current application server
sy-pagno	Current list page
sy-pfkey	Current GUI status
sy-prdsn	Spool file during list printout
sy-repid	Current ABAP program
sy-saprl	Current release number
sy-scols	Width of current screen
sy-slset	Current selection screen variant
sy-spono	Spool number at list printout
sy-srows	Height of current screen
sy-staco	First displayed column at list event
sy-staro	Uppermost displayed list line at list event
sy-stepl	Current line in a table control
sy-subrc	Return value of an ABAP statement
sy-sysid	Name of the current ABAP system

sy-tabix	Current table index
sy-tcode	Current transaction code
sy-tfill	Number of lines in the current internal table
sy-timlo	Local time of the current user
sy-title	Title of the current dynpro
sy-tleng	Line width in the current internal table
sy-tvar0	Value for 1st placeholder in list or column heading
sy-tvar1	Value for 2nd placeholder in list or column heading
sy-tvar2	Value for 3rd placeholder in list or column heading
sy-tvar3	Value for 4th placeholder in list or column heading
sy-tvar4	Value for 5th placeholder in list or column heading
sy-tvar5	Value for 6th placeholder in list or column heading
sy-tvar6	Value for 7th placeholder in list or column heading
sy-tvar7	Value for 8th placeholder in list or column heading
sy-tvar8	Value for 9th placeholder in list or column heading
sy-tvar9	Value for 10th placeholder in list or column heading
sy-tzone	Time difference to UTC reference time
sy-ucomm	Current function code
sy-uline	Horizontal line for lists
sy-uname	Logon name of current user
sy-uzeit	Local time of the current SAP system
sy-vline	Vertical line for lists
sy-wtitl	Displays standard titles of the basic list.
sy-zonlo	Time zone of the current user

Table 5: Predefined Designators

The following table lists predefined designators for specific operands.

Name	Meaning
constructor	Instance constructor
class-constructor	Static constructor
super	Pseudo-reference variable for the direct superclass
table_line	Pseudo-component for the entire line of an internal table

Table 6: Built-In Functions

The following table lists the implicitly existing functions.

Name	Meaning
`abs( ... )`	Absolute value
`acos( ... )`	Arc cosine
`asin( ... )`	Arc sine
`atan( ... )`	Arc tangent
`ceil( ... )`	Next integer
`cos( ... )`	Cosine
`cosh( ... )`	Hyperbolic cosine
`charlen( ... )`	Length of a character (as of Release 6.10)
`dbmaxlen( ... )`	Maximum length of a string of external type RAWSTRING, SSTRING or STRING (as of Release 6.10)
`exp( ... )`	Exponential function
`floor( ... )`	Previous integer
`frac( ... )`	Decimal fraction
`lines( ... )`	Number of lines in an internal table (as of Release 6.10)
`log( ... )`	Natural logarithm
`log10( ... )`	Logarithm to the base 10
`numofchar( ... )`	Number of characters with single counting of non-Unicode double-byte codes (as of Release 6.10)
`sign( ... )`	Sign function
`sin( ... )`	Sine
`sinh( ... )`	Hyperbolic sine
`sqrt( ... )`	Square root
`strlen( ... )`	Number of characters with double counting of non-Unicode double-byte codes
`tan( ... )`	Tangent
`tanh( ... )`	Hyperbolic tangent
`trunc( ... )`	Integral fraction
`xstrlen( ... )`	Number of bytes (as of Release 6.10)

Table 7: Selectors

The following table lists the selectors and operators that can be specified as parts of designators.

Selector/ Operator	Meaning
-	Structure component selector
->	Object component selector
=>	Class component selector
~	Interface component selector, column selector
->*	Dereferencing operator for data references

Table 8: Boolean Operators

The following table lists the Boolean operators used to link and negate logical expressions.

Operator	Meaning
AND	AND operation
OR	OR operation
NOT	Negation

Table 9: Literals

The following table lists the literals that can be used in ABAP source code.

Syntax	Meaning
'...'	Text field literal of type c with up to 255 characters
\`...\`	String literal of type string with up to 255 characters (as of Release 6.10)
[+|-]...	Numeric literal of type i or p with up to 31 digits

Table 10: Additional Special Characters in ABAP

The following table lists additional special characters that can be used in ABAP statements and that haven't been listed among the ABAP statements.

Character	Meaning
.	End of a statement
=	Assignment operator
?=	Casting operator
*	Line comment

"	End-of-line comment
!	Escape character for operands
+(...)	Indication of offset/length after operands

Special Characters in Regular Expressions

As of Release 7.0, ABAP supports extended regular expressions according to POSIX standard 1003.2. The implementation is based on the Boost Regex Library. Copyright (c) 1998-2004 Dr. John Maddock.

A regular expression is a pattern made up of literals and special characters that describes a set of strings. Regular expressions can be used after the `REGEX` addition of the ABAP statements `FIND` and `REPLACE` in order to perform string searches.

The following tables summarize the special characters of regular expressions.

Table 11: Escape Character

Special character	Meaning
\	Escape character for special characters

Tabelle 12: Special Characters for Single-Character Patterns

Sonderzeichen	Meaning
.	Placeholder for any single character
\C	Placeholder for any single character
\d	Placeholder for any digit
\D	Placeholder for any non-digit
\l	Placeholder for any lowercase letter
\L	Placeholder for any non-lowercase letter
\s	Placeholder for a blank space
\S	Placeholder for a non-blank space
\u	Placeholder for any uppercase letter
\U	Placeholder for any non-uppercase letter
\w	Placeholder for any alphanumeric character including "_"
\W	Placeholder for any non-alphanumeric character except for "_"

Tables

[ ]	Definition of a value set for single characters
[^]	Negation of a value set for single characters
[-]	Definition of an area within a value set for single characters
[[:alnum:]]	Notation for all alphanumeric characters within a value set
[[:alpha:]]	Notation for all letters within a value set
[[:blank:]]	Notation for blank space and horizontal tabulator within a value set
[[:cntrl:]]	Notation for all control characters within a value set
[[:digit:]]	Notation for all digits within a value set
[[:graph:]]	Notation for all graphical characters within a value set
[[:lower:]]	Notation for all lowercase letters within a value set
[[:print:]]	Notation for all displayable characters within a value set
[[:punct:]]	Notation for all punctuation mark characters within a value set
[[:space:]]	Notation for all blank spaces, tabulators, and carriage feeds within a value set
[[:unicode:]]	Notation for all Unicode characters whose code exceeds 255 characters, within a value set
[[:upper:]]	Notation for all uppercase letters within a value set
[[:word:]]	Notation for all alphanumeric characters plus "_" within a value set
[[:xdigit:]]	Notation for all hexadecimal digits within a value set
\a \f \n \r \t \v	Various platform-specific control characters
[..]	Reserved for future enhancements
[==]	Reserved for future enhancements

Table 13: Special Characters for String Patterns

Special character	Meaning
{n}	String of n single characters
{n,m}	String of at least n and not exceeding m single characters
{n,m}?	Reserved for future enhancements
?	One or no single character
*	String of any number of single characters including no character

*?	Reserved for future enhancements
+	String of any number of single characters excluding no character
+?	Reserved for future enhancements
|	Linkage of two alternative expressions
( )	Definition of subgroups with registration
(?:)	Definition of subgroups without registration
\1, \2, \3 ...	Placeholder for subgroup registers
\Q ... \E	Definition of a string of literals
(? ...)	Reserved for future enhancements

Table 14: Special Characters for Search Patterns

Special character	Meaning
^	Anchor character for the beginning of a line
\A	Anchor character for the beginning of a string
$	Anchor character for the end of a line
\Z	Anchor character for the end of a string
\<	Beginning of a word
\>	End of a word
\b	Beginning or end of a word
\B	Space between characters within a word
(?=)	Forecast condition
(?!)	Negated forecast condition

Table 15: Special Characters for Replacement Texts

Special character	Meaning
$0, $&	Placeholder for the entire found location
$1, $2, $3...	Placeholder for subgroup registers
$`	Placeholder for the text preceding the found location
$'	Placeholder for the text after the found location

Dynpro Statements

This part lists all statements of the dynpro flow logic in alphabetical order. Obsolete statements and additions are not listed.

CALL SUBSCREEN

Syntax

```
CALL SUBSCREEN sub_area [INCLUDING prog dynnr].
```

Effect

Integrates a subscreen into the subscreen area `sub_area` of the current dynpro or of a tabstrip control and calls the subscreen flow logic.

Additions

- `INCLUDING prog dynnr`
  Identifies the subscreen `dynnr` of a program `prog` to be integrated at PBO. At PAI, the dynpro flow logic of the subscreen integrated at PBO is called without this addition.

CHAIN

Syntax

```
CHAIN.
  ...
ENDCHAIN.
```

Effect

Defines a processing chain that enables a common processing of all dynpro fields specified after `FIELD` statements.

FIELD

Syntax

```
FIELD dynp_field
  { [ MODULE mod [ {ON INPUT}
                 | {ON REQUEST}
                 | {ON *-INPUT}
```

Dynpro

```
                    | {ON {CHAIN-INPUT|CHAIN-REQUEST}}
                    | {AT CURSOR-SELECTION} ] ]
    | [ [MODULE mod] WITH hlp ] }.
```

Effect

Controls the data transport for dynpro field dynp_field from the dynpro to the ABAP program during the PAI event. For POH and POV field or input, helps are called for dynp_field without any data transport.

Additions

- MODULE mod
  Calls dialog module mod which can contain input checks for PAI and field or input helps for POH and POV for dynp_field.
- ON INPUT
  Calls the dialog module only if dynpro field dynp_field is not empty.
- ON REQUEST
  Calls the dialog module only if dynpro field dynp_field has been changed since PBO.
- ON *-INPUT
  Calls the dialog module only if the first character entered into dynpro field dynp_field was a "*" character and if the field has the specific *-**Input** attribute.
- ON {CHAIN-INPUT|CHAIN-REQUEST}
  Calls the dialog module within CHAIN—ENDCHAIN only if the ON INPUT or ON REQUEST conditions are met for all dynpro fields specified after FIELD in the current string.
- AT CURSOR-SELECTION
  Calls the dialog module only for a function "CS" of type "S" and only if the cursor is positioned at an input or output field of the screen.
- [MODULE mod] WITH hlp
  Displays the additional data-element documentation specified in hlp when the field help for dynpro field dynp_field is called. The hlp field can be provided in dialog module mod.

LOOP

Syntax

```
LOOP [AT itab [INTO wa]
              [CURSOR top_line] [FROM n1] [TO n2]]
     WITH CONTROL contrl.
  ...
ENDLOOP.
```

Effect

Defines a loop that is linked with a table control `contrl` via `WITH CONTROL`.

Addition

- `AT itab [INTO wa]`
  Initiates parallel sequential processing of table internal table `itab` of the corresponding ABAP program at PBO and PAI. In this context, `wa` serves as an interface work area for the table control. At PAI, the process is then executed without the `WITH CONTROL` addition.
- `CURSOR top_line`
  Controls at PBO the line of the internal table `itab` in which the processing of the table begins.
- `[FROM n1] [TO n2]`
  Restricts the lines of the internal table `itab` at the time of PBO to those that are between `n1` and/or `n2`.

MODULE

Syntax

```
MODULE mod [AT {EXIT-COMMAND|CURSOR-SELECTION}]
           [ON {CHAIN-INPUT|CHAIN-REQUEST}]
           [SWITCH switch].
```

Effect

Calls a dialog module `mod` in the corresponding ABAP program.

Additions

- `AT EXIT-COMMAND`
  Calls the dialog module for a function of type "E".

- `AT CURSOR-SELECTION`
  Calls the dialog module only for a function "CS" of type "S" and only if the cursor is positioned at an input or output field of the screen.

- `ON {CHAIN-INPUT|CHAIN-REQUEST}`
  Calls the dialog module within `CHAIN—ENDCHAIN` only if the `ON INPUT` or `ON REQUEST` conditions are met for all dynpro fields specified after `FIELD` in the current processing chain.

Addition since Release 7.0

- `SWITCH switch`
  Calls the dialog module only if status of the switch specified by `switch` is "on".

PROCESS

Syntax

```
PROCESS { {BEFORE OUTPUT}
        | {AFTER INPUT}
        | {ON HELP-REQUEST}
        | {ON VALUE-REQUEST} }.
```

Effect

Initiates event blocks whose events are triggered at certain times during the dynpro processing.

Additions

- `BEFORE OUTPUT`
  Point in time before a dynpro screen is sent to the presentation layer.

- `AFTER INPUT`
  User action in the user interface that is linked to a function code.

- `ON HELP-REQUEST`
  Request for a field help (F1).

- `ON VALUE-REQUEST`
  Request for an input help (F4).

ST Statements

In this section you will find all statements of ST (Simple Transformation), SAP's proprietary transformation language, in alphabetical order. Since Release 6.40, ST programs can be called using the `CALL TRANSFORMATION` statement in order to transform ABAP data into XML and vice versa. During the call ABAP data objects are tied to the data roots of the main template of the called transformation. For more detailed information, please refer to **http://help.sap.com • Documentation • SAP NetWeaver • Application Platform • ABAP Technology • ABAP Programming and Runtime Environment (BC-ABA) • External Programming Interfaces • Simple Transformations**.

ST programs are XML documents that consist of literal elements and ST commands. ST commands differ from literal elements (XML elements, attributes, and text) by their namespace, *http://www.sap.com/transformation-templates*, for which the prefix `tt` is used as a convention.

The structure of an ST program consists of optional declarations, one main template, and optional sub-templates which can also contain declarations. Templates are patterns used by the XML document into which ABAP data is serialized or from which data is deserialized.

```
<?sap.transform simple?>
<tt:transform [template="tmpl"]
        xmlns:tt="http://www.sap.com/transformation-templates">
  [<tt:type name="type1" [...] />
   <tt:type name="type2" [...] />
   ...]
  [<tt:root name="root1" [...] />
   <tt:root name="root2" [...] />
   ...]
  [<tt:parameter name="para1" [...] />
   <tt:parameter name="para2" [...] />
   ...]
  [<tt:variable name="vari1" [...] />
   <tt:variable name="vari2" [...] />
   ...]
```

```
  <tt:template [name="tmpl1"]>
    ...
  </tt:template>
  [<tt:template [name="tmpl2"]>
    ...
   </tt:template>
   ...]
</tt:transform>
```

Within tt:transform the order of elements is arbitrary.

apply

Syntax

```
<tt:apply name="tmpl" [ref="node"]>
  ...
</tt:apply>
```

Effect

Calls a subtemplate tmpl. The element can contain the commands tt:with-root and tt:with-parameter.

Addition

- ref
  Sets the root node of the tree structure of the called subtemplate to node node instead of the current node.

assign

Syntax

```
<tt:assign [to-ref="to_node"|to-var="to_vari"]
           [ref="node"|val="value"|var="vari"] />
```

Effect

Assigns to a data root to_node, to a variable or to a parameter to_vari the value of a current node, the value of a node node, the value value (see Table 16), or the value of a variable or of a parameter vari.

attribute

Syntax

```
<tt:attribute name="attr" [ref="node"]>
  ...
</tt:attribute>
```

Effect

Defines a non-literal attribute `attr` of the current XML element.

Addition

- `ref`
  Sets the current node to `node`, in connection with the non-literal attribute.

call

Syntax

```
<tt:call transformation="trafo">
  ...
</tt:call>
```

Effect

Calls another ST program `trafo`. The element can contain the commands `tt:with-root` and `tt:with-parameter`.

clear

Syntax

```
<tt:clear [ref="node"|var="vari"] />
```

Effect

Initializes the current node.

Additions

- `ref`
  Initializes node `node` instead of the current node.
- `var`
  Initializes the variable or parameter `vari` instead of the current node.

ST

cond

Syntax

```
<tt:[s-|d-]cond
            [using="precond"]
            [data="assertion"]
            [[s-|d-]check="cond"]>
  ...
</tt:[s-|d-]cond>
```

Effect

Defines a condition for nodes that is relevant for serialization, deserialization or both.

Additions

- `using`
  Specifies a precondition `precond` (see Table 17).
- `data`
  Specifies an assertion `assertion` (see Table 18).
- `[s-|d-]check`
  Specifies a condition `cond` (see Table 19) for serialization, deserialization or both.

cond-var

Syntax

```
<tt:cond-var check="cond">
  ...
</tt:cond-var>
```

Effect

Defines a condition for variables.

Additions

- `check`
  Specifies a condition `cond` for serialization and deserialization.

context

Syntax

```
<tt:context> ... </tt:context>
```

Effect
Defines a context for local data declarations with `root`, `variable` and `parameter` commands in subtemplates.

copy

Syntax

```
<tt:copy [ref="node"] />
```

Effect
Serializes ABAP data objects into asXML format or deserializes the asXML format.

Addition

- `ref`
  Sets the current node of the command to `node`.

deserialize

Syntax

```
<tt:deserialize> ... </tt:deserialize>
```

Effect
Restricts a section of the template to deserialization.

empty

Syntax

```
<tt:empty />
```

Effect
Defines an empty pattern for deserialization within a condition `cond`.

ST

extensible

Syntax

```
<... tt:extensible="on"|"deep-static"|"deep-dynamic"
                      |"off"|"deep-off" ...>
  ...
</...>
```

Release
7.0

Effect
Skips literal elements of the input stream during deserialization, which are not specified in the ST program.

front

Syntax

```
<tt:front> ... </tt:front>
```

Release
7.0

Effect
Defines the first components of a structure in a type definition with `tt:type`. The element can contain `tt:node` commands.

group

Syntax

```
<tt:group> ... </tt:group>
```

Effect
Combines conditions into a group. The element can contain `tt:[s-|d-]cond` commands.

include

Syntax

```
<tt:include name="trafo" [templates="tmpl1 tmpl2 ..."] />
```

Effect
Includes another ST program `trafo`.

Addition

- `templates="tmpl1 tmpl2 ..."`
  Restricts the templates to be included to `tmpl1`, `tmpl2`, ...

lax

Syntax

```
<... tt:lax="on"|"off"|"deep-on"|"deep-off" ...>
  ...
</...>
```

Effect

Determines whether the name of a literal element may deviate from the input stream during deserialization.

loop

Syntax

```
<tt:loop [ref="node"] [name="alias"]>
  ...
</tt:loop>
```

Effect

Transforms an internal table.

Additions

- `ref`
  Sets the current node of the command to `node`.
- `name`
  Defines an alias name `alias` for the current node in the loop.

namespace

Syntax

```
<tt:namespace name="prefix"/>
```

Effect

Declares a namespace within a literal element.

node

Syntax

```
<tt:node name="node" [[line-]type="type"
                      [length="len"]
```

ST

```
                              [decimals="dec"]]
                             [extensible="on"|"deep-static"
                                        |"deep-dynamic"|"off"
                                        |"deep-off"]>
  ...
</tt:node>
```

Release

7.0

Effect

Defines a component `node` of a structure in a type definition using `tt:type`. The element can contain additional `tt:node` commands.

Additions

- `[line-]type`
  Specifies a type from the ABAP dictionary, from a type pool, from a global class or via `?` a generic type. `line` defines a table with this line type.
- `length`
  Specifies the length.
- `decimals`
  Specifies the fractional portions.
- `extensible`
  Restricts the number of components of the structure to the components defined in the ST program.

parameter

Syntax

```
<tt:parameter name="para" [kind="in|out|in/out"]
                          [[s-val="value"][d-val="value"]]
                          |[val="value"] />
```

Effect

Declares a parameter `para` for the main template outside of templates, or declares a local parameter within subtemplates.

Additions

- `kind`
  Defines an input, output, or input/output parameter.

- `[s-|d-]val`
  Specifies a start value `value` (see Table 16) for serialization, deserialization or both.

read

Syntax

```
<tt:read var="vari" type="type"
                    [length="len"]
                    [decimals="dec"]
                    [map="mapping_list"] />
```

Effect

Reads a value from the XML input stream into a variable or a parameter `var`.

Additions

- `type="type" [length="len"] [decimals="dec"]`
  Specifies the expected type.
- `map="mapping_list"`
  Specifies a mapping list `mapping_list` in order to read multiple values at the same time.

ref

Syntax

Element

```
<tt:ref name="node"> ... </tt:ref>
```

Attribute

```
<... tt:ref name="node" ...> ... </...>
```

Effect

Sets the current node in an element `ref` or of a literal element to node `node`.

ST

root

Syntax

```
<tt:root name="root" [[line-]type="type"
                      [length="len"]
                      [decimals="dec"]] />
```

Effect

Declares a data root `root` for the main template outside of templates, or declares a local data root within subtemplates. The data roots of the main template represent the interface between the simple transformation and the ABAP program. The local data roots of sub-templates represent an interface to the calling template.

Additions since Release 7.0

- `[line-]type`
  Specifies a type from the ABAP dictionary, from a type pool, from a global class or via `?` a generic type. `line` defines a table with this line type.
- `length`
  Specifies the length.
- `decimals`
  Specifies the fractional portions.

serialize

Syntax

```
<tt:serialize> ... </tt:serialize>
```

Effect

Restricts a section of the template to serialization.

skip

Syntax

```
<tt:skip [name="name"] [count="cnt"]/>
```

Effect

Skips elements of the input stream during deserialization.

Additions

- `name="name"`
  Specifies the name `name` of the element to be skipped.
- `count="cnt"`
  Specifies the number of elements to be skipped.

switch

Syntax

```
<tt:switch> ... </tt:switch>
```

Effect

Combines conditions into a case list. The element can contain `tt:[s-|d-]cond` commands.

switch-var

Syntax

```
<tt:switch-var> ... </tt:switch-var>
```

Effect

Combines conditions for variables into a case list. The element can contain `tt:cond-var` commands.

template

Syntax

```
<tt:template [name="tmpl"]>
  ...
</tt:template>
```

Effect

Defines a main template or sub-template.

Addition

- `name="tmpl"`
  Specifies a name `tmpl` for the template. A template without a name is always a main template.

text

Syntax

```
<tt:text> ... </tt:text>
```

Effect

Flags a literal text as such even if it contains only empty spaces.

transform

Syntax

```
<tt:transform [template="tmpl"]>
  ...
</tt:transform>
```

Effect

Root element of an ST program.

Addition

- `template="tmpl"`
  Defines the main template of the transformation.

type

Syntax

```
<tt:type name="tname"
  [[line-]type="type"
   [length="len"]
   [decimals="dec"]]
  [extensible="on"|"deep-static"|"deep-dynamic"
              |"off"|"deep-off"]>
  ...
</tt:type>
```

Release

7.0

Effect

Defines a type `tname` outside a template that can be used to type data roots. The element can contain the `tt:front` and `tt:node` commands.

Additions

- `[line-]type`
  Specifies a type from the ABAP dictionary, from a type pool, or from a global class or via `?` a generic type. `line` defines a table with this line type.
- `length`
  Specifies the length.
- `decimals`
  Specifies the fractional portions.
- `extensible`
  Restricts the number of components of a structure to the components defined in the ST program.

value

Syntax

```
<tt:value [ref="node"] [map="mapping_list"] />
```

Effect

Transforms an elementary data object.

Additions

- `ref`
  Sets the current node of the command to `node`.
- `map="mapping_list"`
  Specifies a mapping list `mapping_list` in order to transform multiple values at the same time.

value-ref

Syntax

```
<... tt:value-ref="node" ...>
```

Effect

Short form of `tt:value` within a literal element.

Addition

- `ref`
  Sets the current node of the command to `node`.

variable

Syntax

```
<tt:variable name="vari"
             [[s-val="value"][d-val="value"]]
             |[val="value"] />
```

Effect

Declares a variable `vari` for the main template outside of templates, or declares a local variable within subtemplates.

Addition

- `[s-|d-]val`
  Specifies a start value `value` (see Table 16) for serialization, deserialization or both.

with-parameter

Syntax

```
<tt:with-parameter name="para"
                   [ref="node"|val="value"|var="vari"] />
```

Effect

When calling a template with `tt:apply` or `tt:call`, this addition binds the formal parameter `para` of the called subtemplate or of the main template to the current node, to node `node`, to a value `value` (see Table 16) or to a variable `vari`.

with-root

Syntax

```
<tt:with-root name="root" [ref="node"] />
```

Effect

When calling a template with `tt:apply` or `tt:call`, this addition binds the data root `root` of the called subtemplate to main template to the current node or to node `node`.

write

Syntax

```
<tt:write var="vari" [map="mapping_list"] />
```

Effect

Writes the value of a variable or of a parameter `var` into the target XML document.

Addition

- `map="mapping_list"`
  Specifies a mapping list `mapping_list` in order to write multiple values at the same time.

ST

Tables with ST Information

Table 16: Specification of Values

The following table shows the specification of values value, depending on the related ABAP data type.

ABAP data type	Specification
x, xstring	X('value')
d	D('value')
p	P(value)
f	F(value)
i	I(value) | value
n	N('value')
c, cstring	C('value') | 'value'
t	T('value')

The initial value can always be specified as initial.

Table 17: Preconditions

The following table shows you how to specify a precondition precond in the using attribute of a tt:[s-|d-]cond condition. The precondition is met if an ABAP data object of a specific type is bound to the specified data node dnode.

Syntax	Meaning
exist(dnode)	Tied to the nodal point.
type-C(dnode)	There must be an ABAP data object of type c tied to the node.
type-D(dnode)	There must be an ABAP data object of type d tied to the node.
type-F(dnode)	There must be an ABAP data object of type f tied to the node.
type-I(dnode)	There must be an ABAP data object of type i tied to the node.
type-N(dnode)	There must be an ABAP data object of type n tied to the node.
type-P(dnode)	There must be an ABAP data object of type p tied to the node.
type-T(dnode)	There must be an ABAP data object of type t tied to the node.
type-X(dnode)	There must be an ABAP data object of type x tied to the node.

In some cases node `dnode` can be specified directly as `node`, and it can always be specified as `ref('node')`. Multiple preconditions can be combined into a comma-separated list.

Table 18: Assertions

The following table shows you how to specify an assertion `assertion` in the `data` attribute of a `tt:[s-|d-]cond` condition.

<table>
<tr><th>Syntax</th><th>Meaning</th></tr>
<tr><td><code>initial(dnode|var(vari))</code></td><td>The related data object or the variable is initial.</td></tr>
<tr><td><code>dnode|var(vari) = value</code>
<code>value = dnode|var(vari)</code></td><td>The related data object or the variable has a specific value.</td></tr>
</table>

In some cases node `dnode` can be specified directly as `node`, and it can always be specified as `ref('node')`. Multiple assertions can be combined into a comma-separated list.

Table 19: Conditions

The following table shows you how to specify a condition `cond` in the `check` attribute of a `tt:[s-|d-]cond` condition.

<table>
<tr><th>Syntax</th><th>Meaning</th></tr>
<tr><td><code>exist(dnode)</code></td><td>There must be an ABAP data object bound to the node.</td></tr>
<tr><td><code>initial(dnode|var(vari))</code></td><td>The related ABAP data object or the variable must be initial.</td></tr>
<tr><td><code>not-initial(dnode|var(vari))</code></td><td>The related ABAP data object or the variable must not be initial.</td></tr>
<tr><td><code>dnode|var(vari)|value</code>
<code>=|!=|>|>|>=|≥=</code>
<code>|<|≤=</code>
<code>dnode|var(vari)|value</code></td><td>Comparisons between data nodes, variables, or values</td></tr>
</table>

In some cases node `dnode` can be specified directly as `node`, and it can always be specified as `ref('node')`. Multiple conditions can be negated with `not` and they can be linked using `and` or `or`.

The Author

Horst Keller holds a PhD in physics from the technical university of Darmstadt, Germany. He joined SAP in 1995 after having spent several years involved in research projects in various international institutions. As a knowledge architect within the *SAP NetWeaver Application Server ABAP* group, he is mainly responsible for documentation and rollout of ABAP and ABAP Objects, while at the same time developing the programs for formatting and presenting the ABAP documentation, including the related search algorithms. Horst Keller is the author of the books *ABAP Objects—An Introduction to Programming SAP Applications* (Addison-Wesley Professional, 2002) and *The Official ABAP Reference* (SAP PRESS, 2005). Numerous other publications and workshops on this subject round off his work.